D1372765

The Bill Ballance Hip Handbook of Nifty Moves...

The Bill Ballance Hip Handbook of Nifty Moves...

and How to Cope in Situations of Utter Copelessness

An Emotional Survival Kit for Rampaging Scamps of Romance and Ruthless Rogues; A Lexicon of Surging Love; A Sourcebook for the Snappy; A Syllabus of Sagacity; A Profile in Pungence; A Compendium of Cupidity; A Lurid Journal for Culture Voluptuaries.

Brimming with Half-Aphorisms, All Stated with the Undoubted Omnipotence of a Man who has Paid his Dues. No Ghostwriters Rustle Through these Pages; They Were All Bashed Out on an Elderly Underwood by

Yours with great affection,

Bill Ballance

Bill Ballance

Nash Publishing, Los Angeles

Copyright 1973 © Bill Ballance

All rights reserved. No part of this book
may be reproduced in any form or by any means
without permission in writing from the publisher.

Library of Congress Catalog Card Number: 73-83523
International Standard Book Number: 0-8402-1320-4

Published simultaneously in the United States and Canada
by Nash Publishing Corporation, 9255 Sunset Boulevard,
Los Angeles, California 90069.

Printed in the United States of America.

First Printing.

*To my two ex-wives, without whose absence this book
could never have been written.
For my two dashing and splendid sons,
James Michael Ballance and Kurt Bennett Ballance,
who regarded my activities with indulgent smiles
and faintly amused tolerance.*

Contents

Preface

Preface writing is an occupational disease with authors, but I'm going to lay one on you anyway. Let me state emphatically and briskly right off that *I am eternally grateful to:*

Vernon D. Wood, who has managed my business affairs for more than twenty years and has been my valued friend and philosophical consultant through thin and thin. There are countless crooks, sharpshooters, and fiscal vultures hovering on the periphery of showbiz, men who genuinely feel that the money a performer makes is money that will eventually be *theirs* if they can just arrange to handle it long enough. Woody is the rare exception to that rapscallion rule. *Darwin Lamm,* my brilliant and ambitious personal manager who skillfully orchestrates my career and who firmly believes that I can do anything he puts his greedy mind to. *Ray Stanfield,* outstanding Storer broadcasting executive, without whose indomitable courage and imagination nothing would have happened for me these past three years. *Jim Freeman,* my co-business manager (partner of Wood) who has often saved me from harebrained investments that would have forced me to spend my sunset years rocking furiously on the verandah of the Old Communicators' Home at Mount Glottis. *Mary Bronson,* my faithful and efficient secretary since 1952, a patient lady indeed whose skill is matched only by her loyalty. *Dr. and Mrs. Norton F. Kristy,* warmhearted chums, willing to share with me their accumulated wisdom. *Peter Green,* that irridescent illustrator of this book and designer of its cover, a man whose dry-point wizardry is enough to melt the umber off your palate and set the Wyeth family sobbing aloud with bitter envy. *Katherine Orloff,* brilliant journalist who sifted through more than two thousand work sheets of my daily shows to pluck an occasional testy tidbit. *Jim Storer, Don Page, Peter Lund, Willis Duff, Gary Owens, Chuck Southcott, Casey Kasem, Ted Randal, George Jay, Bob Hudson, Ron Landry, Jim Hawthorne, Don Imus, Chuck Blore, Frank Schooley, Bill Kelley, Dick Clark, Bill Gavin, Ralph Story, Syd Eiges, Maurie Webster*—all of whom have been wrung through the wringers of electronic experience and have evolved into top-drawer communicators and steadfast friends. *My Favorite Girl,* an exquisite creature without whose urgent and insatiable romantic demands this book would have been finished in half the time.

And that reminds me, people are already inquiring, "Is this one of those blatantly sexy publications?" Well, let me put it this way: There are exactly 98 positions you can assume while reading it.

This, then, is your book. These thoughts are for you, these hints and observations are for *your* use. Consider everything within these tear-stained pages to be *your* property from this day forward. Just one thing—I get to keep the money.

Submerged in here is something for most of you and nothing for some of you, but ALL of you will find somewhere within your true secret self impaled like a pinned beetle by a piercing parable, a spiny observation applicable only to your organically grown psyche.

And as you riffle hungrily through the following, remember Ballance's Biblio-Law: A book is man's best friend because a book can be shut up without offense.

Bill Ballance
Hollywood, California
September, 1973

*Half of everything I say in this book
is frivolous, but I say it so that the
other half will reach you.*

The
Bill Ballance
Hip Handbook
of Nifty Moves...

Chapter One
Omniscient Laws,
Half-Aphorisms,
and Addlepated Axioms

Before I enfilade you with homespun philosophy and cracker-barrel wisdom, I want to emphasize that you are not dealing with just any rookie hoodwinker. In this era of revolutionary chatter, wet-eyed limousine liberals, mysticism, and daydreams, I submit a few hard facts. My stern laws are bold and commanding formulations reached after debilitating decades of rueful reflection about the world of the mind and the deeply involved heart. At first my laws were received with widespread public apathy, but now they're accepted with tumultuous torpor and a thunderous smattering of applause.

If your life is one of progressive deterioration and dismal daily dreads, join me now; let me take you by your tiny, clenched koala-bear hands. If you feel you're about to become a harness case, what you need is a little emotional order, a little direction, and the shared knowledge of corrugated sledding to release that loving potential simmering on the back burner of your psyche.

These vaporous guidelines were requested by the Senior Lobotomy Surgeons at the Whamo Neuropsychiatric Institute of Levitation and Competitive Persecution Traumas and by a desperate group of RNs (Resident Nymphs) at the Breaking Point Clinic for those in the Fast Lane for Flipsville, home of the fleecelined straitjacket with thirty-four luminous buckles that glow in the dark and spell out: "I AM *NOT* NUTS. I AM *RAISINS.*"

So if you are whipsawed by praise and blame and paralyzing bouts of indecision and you feel you're heading for the State Home for the Quaint, about to win the Nobel Prize for Masochism, seething with inner resentment, plagued by vertiginous neuroses and unruly disoriented inner visions, we are now officially *psychopathic soulmates.* Read on and *commence to cope!*

Laws and Women

Let me begin this chapter by clarifying laws and women. There ought to be more of both. It's gruntbrained to speak of "superiority" of one sex over the other; each sex has what the other has not; each sex completes the other, and is completed by the other. They are nothing alike, but the happiness of both depends on each asking and receiving from the other what only the other can give. I won't delve into deviants here; also, I am not interested in helping the kind of woman who wears a saran-wrap turban to preserve her sanity and keep her head from spoiling. Such gnarled and twisted women are out; those psyched-out uptight hoydens with a hideous lust for inflicting excruciating torment are beyond repair, and also this chapter. These laws are a kind of confrontation therapy, which depends on creative communicative psychodrama and a willingness to participate in my encounter workshop. So here we go, and remember, "All is well if we touch and tell." Bill Ballance here, apprentice eccentric and latent swashbuckler, calling the shots:

It is written that attractiveness in a woman is based on her *appearance* almost exclusively, whereas a man's attractiveness is predicated on power, success, potency of personality, and an ability to move things in this world. If a man achieves this level of competence, women tend to see him as sexually appealing, regardless of appearance and age. Where a witty woman is a treasure, a witty beauty is a power. Beauty is the first gift nature gives to a woman, and beauty is also the first gift that nature takes away. Hence, a beautiful woman dies twice—the first time, when her looks begin to fade. Still, it is Ballance's Pneumatic Bosom Law that a girl may be both ignorant and she may be shapely, but she is never ignorant of the fact that she is shapely. A corollary is that a calculating girl works with figures; especially her own. And, in most women, bosoms and brains are inversely proportional. So here we have Ballance's Academic Effect: If a woman is good looking, higher education is unnecessary. If she isn't good looking, higher education is inadequate.

Another law that pertains to this situation is Ballance's Escape Axiom: Behind every successful man is a woman he managed, somehow, to get away from. Incidentally, girls, don't always insist on knowing everything your man is thinking. Don't keep probing and prying. Give the guy a break, and don't try to share his every waking thought. Remember Ballance's Law of Personal Intrusion: Women who study their men incessantly, who try to read them like books, will soon wear out their bindings.

Incidentally, Ballance's Laryngeal Law comes briskly into play here, reminding you that anytime a woman suffers in silence, she'll have plenty to say about it later. A woman simply cannot learn to be wise any more than she can learn to be beautiful. That's one of the reasons why half of the women in

Women who study their men incessantly, who try to read them like books, will soon wear out their bindings.

the world are unhappy. They're sick and nervous because they can't have those things that are making the other half unhappy. But you show me a woman who always has her two feet firmly planted on the ground and I'll show you a woman who has to put her pantyhose on over her head.

The oldest plastic in the world is still a love-stricken man in the hands of a predatory woman, which means that it is never prudent to make light of a woman's dark hint. An exception to this palsied postulate is the blind date. When someone says, "She's not really beautiful but she has a great personality and a fine mind," that means she's an authentic dog with fat ankles. It is known as Ballance's Law of Unified Opposites that a homely blind date is always virtuous to the point of eccentricity, due to the fact that she was molested as a child of twenty-eight.

It is Ballance's Law of Anticipation that it is always wise to support Girl Scout cookies. After all, today's Brownie is to-morrow's cupcake. Speaking of children, it is an Addlepated Axiom that it is far better to have loved and lost than to have to buy a batch of bassinets and do the homework for six kids.

By the way, never be critical of a woman because of her hyperdemure, subdued manner. I've learned over the years that it's always those quiet, introverted girls who are the niftiest, most frenzied kind of lovers.

It is written that flirting is the gentle art of making a man feel pleased with himself, and a corollary is that while every woman has her price, some hold bargain sales. A favorite remark of mine along these lines is that many a girl gets first-hand infor-mation in a second-hand car, probably at the Busy-Hands-are-Happy-Hands Drive-In Movie. Which, in turn, is much better than the woman who uses booze as a substitute for love and as a consolation for loneliness. It is Ballance's Law of Feminine Wiles that a smart girl never shows her hand until she has her man ready to eat out of it. Thus, the clever lady doesn't develop inferiority feelings when she is ignored by an electric-eye door opener.

A really wise woman always makes a slow guy think he's a fast operator, and a sharp girl doesn't have to know anything about archery to keep her lover in a quiver. But don't get your lover so uptight that he becomes high-strung and needs a fistful of tranquilizers just to feed his goldfish. The idea is to keep the way to your girlish heart open through a large pulsating artery connected to your guy's wallet.

Should your enthusiasm dwindle, it is known as the Ballance Law of Obtuse Motives that when a woman is bored with her man, she always says to him, "I think we should both see other *people*"; she never says, "I want to meet *new guys*," or, "You should meet *new girls.*" It's always, "I think we should both see *other people.*" Somehow the phrase seems more wholesomely gregarious instead of just random horny.

A lovable philosopher in his middle-earlies, probably myself, once observed that when a woman says she wants to "go out and get a job to express herself, and make use of her educational background and find out who she really is," it generally means that she is hopelessly behind with her ironing. This problem can be quickly solved, however, through application of the Ballance Law of Extension: It is written, if you give a woman enough rope, she'll hang another clothesline in the bathroom (or she'll do something knotty).

For you studs out there in a position to hire a woman helper, remember that a legal secretary is one who is over eighteen years old, and that through Ballance's Law of Interactive Tyranny, all women expect and enjoy a certain amount of stern domination. And if things don't happen to run with nimble precision and picturesque smoothness, just recall that any woman who turns out as you expected is not driving a car.

Never forget—a clever man tells a woman he understands her; a stupid man tries to prove it.

For you girls out there who feel like a smudge in a slate-grey world, just remember it is written as Ballance's Law that you never learn anything from good times. You learn only from rough times—when you pit yourself against the hostile world. So hang in there with rechristened eyes and stop wallowing in all those morbid reflections. Take a head-on view of life's

realities, and allow Bill to perpetrate further philosophical out-
rages on your tousled girlish head.

And if you can't stand necking, sit down.

> *A woman is only as old as she looks to the*
> *man who likes to look at her; a man is only*
> *as old as the woman he feels.*

Laws and Men

This section is for those semi-executives of the mid echelon who
suffer from alternating strong effects of the humiliation of
obedience and the ecstasy of command. We must begin by
acknowledging the primal Ballance Law that states, "He who
stoops to conquer, conquers only stoops." And I think it perti-
nent to mention that the *second half* of a man's life is made up
of nothing but the habits he's accumulated during the first half.

Basically, the essential super-trendy problem in "success"
with women, is persuading them to go the distance. There are
laws, however, such as Ballance's Rule of Fine Feathered
Fillies: One man's gift is another man's grouse, and these
warrant your wee span of attention. To be popular with girls, a
man has to know when to do the wrong things at exactly the
right time. You must realize that the most accurate evaluation
of a man is somewhere between the opinions of his mother, his
wife, and his secretary.

Still, many a young guy, while browsing through his girl's
family photo album, has failed to heed its warning; it isn't long
before he learns that the only prize that gets bigger after he's
won it is the prize he won at the altar. And if he asks advice of

the already trapped, he should soon recognize Ballance's Law of Divine Recollection: When a man talks about the good old days, he really means the nights. In this complex situation it is best to be tactful. Tact, of course, is the ability to arrive at conclusions without expressing them. Don't be too hasty in solving your greasy little dilemmas. Just remember Ballance's Law of Excessive Haste: The momentary impulsive solution to a problem always contains the seeds of another problem. Utilize the art of conversation, which is telling people a little less than they really want to know, and rest secure in the knowledge that virtue is both its own punishment and insufficient temptation.

While in hot pursuit (a male on the trail of a frail), it is best to remember that appearances are always important. Ballance's Law of Spontaneous Wrinkles can be applied here: A lot of aging males grow old before their time trying to look young after their time. Pretty soon you look as if you're the world's first living brain donor. Also, for those of you with sons, Ballance's Law of Subtle Tracks will eventually apply: The footsteps a boy follows are most likely to be those his father thought he'd covered up.

As you married guys will agree, it's not who you are that counts, it's how your wife found out. Appearances and precedent are important, but your true character is your personality, plus what you've been caught at. This is my Law of the Soft Snare.

You are the architect of your own disaster, and, through Ballance's Law of Revolving Reprobates, it is clear that a man cannot fall in love with a whirlwind without reaping destruction. Still, it is pointless to carry prudence to the point of immobility. Ballance's Corollary of Spare Change says that a prudent man is one who loves within his income, so don't overextend yourselves, guys, or you'll find yourself sheepishly grinning your way to bankruptcy.

It is painfully obvious that gruntheads flourish like crabgrass on our olive drab lawns, so I give you Ballance's Law of Reciprocal Osculation: Being suave is the art of pretending you like the girl more than you like the kiss. And as a well-puckered sequel, it is written that a kiss should never be planned. It should be entirely spontaneous, like a coronary.

Don't go through life as a gutless wonder—remember that backbone in a man is what charm is in a woman.

I always feel selfish spreadeagled alone in my kingsized bed when there are people all over the world sleeping on the ground, so in a spasm of heavy-lidded compassion, I allow certain complaisant ladies between my all-weather percales, but they must always be single, for this is, indeed, Ballance's Self-Preservative Law: A man cannot have his cake and someone else's cookie, too, lest he end up with a crummy situation. Also, when confronted with such a dreary set of stale alternatives, it is written that any man who hides behind a woman's skirts these days isn't a coward, he's a magician. But reputations are earned, not bestowed. For example, no man is master in his own house if his bedroom is painted pink. And a man is indeed lucky if his woman calls him *Ku Klux* because he's a wizard in the sheets.

Unfortunately, the life of every man is a diary in which he means to write one story and writes another instead; and an autobiography does nothing more than reveal the way a man wished he had lived. But I never fault a man for failing repeatedly, as long as he doesn't make the same mistakes over and over in the repeated-pattern syndrome. In fact, I'd rather hire a man who has failed repeatedly, because at least it shows he tried. A man's real worth lies in intangibles—vision, skill, determination, and self-discipline.

It is Ballance's Law of Corrective Surgery that a man never knows what he can *do* until he tries to *un*do what he's already done. A good scare is worth more to a man than all the advice in the world. Look within your head and heart, study your real motives. Remember—the cuckoo who is onto himself is halfway out of the clock.

Any woman will believe you, for example, when you tell her she's the first girl you ever made love to if you happen to be the first liar she's ever met. Still, you have to be patient. Remember the profound words of Madman Maceration, the Smiling Poul-

It is written that a kiss should never be planned, it should be entirely spontaneous, like a coronary.

tryman: If you want a hen to lay, you've got to put up with her cackling. And if that hen drops an egg while straddling her nest, my friend, count yourself lucky indeed, for she has just given you a Standing Ovulation. But a word to the man who prefers anonymous fat women when he makes love to a random porker; that man is taking pot luck.

Men, you must also learn to compromise with your girl. Remember Ballance's Law: A woman will always forgive you if you confess you're all wrong. In addition, I have for you a whimsical maxim, should you carry things too far: If a man really wants to write something that will live forever, he should sign a mortgage.

At the bottom of all this is Ballance's Convoluted Conclusion: A man can never understand a woman as much as he loves her. This fact can, however, be offset by Ballance's Law of Total Exasperation: Often, it is easier to change your girl than to change her mind.

Women the weaker sex? Listen, it takes six men to carry *a man to his grave and only* one *woman to* put *him there.*

Laws of Character and Personality

Let us begin with Ballance's Law of Judgment: Most people are unsure of their own instincts; they want reassurance, so they ask someone else whether they should like a particular person or not. And because the world loves bad news, they nearly always get a negative answer, or at least a carefully qualified one. This is known as insecurity, born of the age of the four A's: Anxiety, Apprehension, and Agonizing Aspirations.

The worst possible thing that can happen is to accommodate

your personality to *self-pity,* which is easily the most destructive of the nonpharmaceutical narcotics; it is addictive, gives momentary pleasure, and separates the victim from reality. We will therefore proceed, attempting either to eliminate or reverse this process. Face it, chums, you must prioritize the things that really count and forget the things that don't. Always ask yourself—what's to be *gained* by it?

Everyone becomes a child when confronted with authority, but the most important thing to remember is: Never give in to a sense of fear. It is a Ballance Law that fear creates aggressiveness, and that aggressiveness engenders hostility, which in turn generates more fear. It's a disastrous, vicious circle. Don't let it get to you, but don't always expect to be deliriously happy, either. It is written that you must have sorrow to balance joy or you get so you don't know one from the other.

Even though character is what a human being is when he thinks no one can see what he's doing, it also encompasses poise, which, of course, is the ability to be ill at ease naturally. It is a basic fact of life that no matter how many troublesome problems you may have, you'd be much better off without them. But we all have our ups and downs, so just remember that only a mediocre person is always at his best.

Character is not made in a crisis, it is revealed. It is axiomatic, Ballancewise, that you should always tell it like it is and imagine how it can be. Just be sure to avoid sentimentality, which is unearned emotion. Speaking of emotion, personality can be quickly revealed through the difference between a prejudice and a conviction. You can explain a conviction without getting mad. So strive to be like a watch: Open face, busy hands, well-regulated, and full of good works.

Good breeding consists in concealing how much we think of ourselves and how little we think of others, and it is a penetrating parable that it always pays to be sincere, whether you mean it or not. Watch out for creeps full of moral indignation, though, because what you're dealing with there is simply jealousy with a halo.

For you high-strung types, it is a Ballance Neurasthenic Law that tension and nervousness are the penalties you pay for being a race horse instead of a cow. Likewise, for those of you who are shy, I want you to know that I empathize completely. Shyness is the most personal of all emotions; it depends upon what you are shy *of.*

The way of the world is often callous, and it is a Ballance Law that the strong take it away from the weak, and the smart take it away from the strong. Man copes, and to each situation he brings resources from his past, organized in patterns which have helped him cope before. He copes with a situation not only as a structure of realities, but also as a construction of his perception. It is written that every human being thinks he is not fully understood, and that he has far greater possibilities. Still, you can't keep a madman down, and thanks to Ballance's Law of Logical Limitation the best way to live happily ever after is not to be after too much.

So hold yourself together with determination; remember that only a relentless will can take the place of a broken heart. I can say such things with authority because of my own character—I happen to be brave, dashing, and romantic, with just a touch of the nincompoop (that's a Poop with an income). A wise old philosopher, it may well have been I, the Santayana of Nietzsche Street, once remarked that wisdom is the scar tissue of intelligence. Well, you better believe it, pal, because people who think they know it all enrage those of us who really do. And if you feel that you have a special talent, don't let it lie fallow, be sure to exercise it. Remember Ballance's Immutable Law of Utility—any ability unused will use you.

I am a man of my time and I know it. I'm not expecting eternal fame, because humor operates on the Ballance Principle of Diminishing Renown. It so happens that I sold my soul to the devil in exchange for a peek at the year 2200. I was dismayed to find that not only were my shows and this book forgotten, but I myself was thought to be fictitious. I had hoped to be remembered as the Demosthenes of Drollery. Well, tough totems.

Humor is not meant to be everlasting—in fact, humor is the

world's most perishable commodity. At its best, it is meant to provide an insight into the here and now, and the memory of a reader or listener is as short-lived as the span of a butterfly that has died prematurely. Humor ferments with age into a sour, painful irony.

Humor, like no other art, is totally social in its intent, but unless humor is prepared and served quickly it will collapse like a soufflé. Its function is limited, but its effect can be enormous. Emerson said: "If you would *rule* the world, you must keep it amused." He also said, "A rolling stone gathers momentum," but that was after he opened the Ralph Waldo Emerson Massage Emporium and Tattoo Parlor and has no bearing here, so please don't bring it up again.

People never joke about what makes them happy or what is sacred to them; they joke only about what frightens them or disturbs them—so, if you want to really know someone's character and personality, study his humor. But beware the comedienne. With the exception of Carol Burnett, you rarely find a girl who is pretty and funny at the same time; usually if a girl is funny, it's because she's unattractive, and being a comic is her way of attracting attention and seeking approval.

Comedy is life in a long shot, and tragedy is life in a closeup; the man who sees the consistency in things is a wit, the man who sees the inconsistency in things is a humorist, and the man who can identify and resolve incongruities is a comedian. True wit is the matching of mismatches, and most comedy is partly cruel—which is why we like it (i.e., "I got my first laugh when my mother entered me in a baby contest . . . I was so homely, they used to diaper my face. . . .") You bought this magnificent best seller for one reason—you want me to take you just one subtle, savage step over the brink into inanity. OK, come along peacefully and when something said is funny check its specific levity, search it for Hidden Truth and submerged verities.

> *Modesty is the gentle art of enhancing*
> *your charm by pretending not to be*
> *aware of it.*

Laws of Life

The greatest secret of life, is to spend it on something that will outlast it. Creativeness is the only way you can confirm your immortality. In other words, live as if you were going to die tomorrow, but learn as if you were going to live forever. It is a Ballance Law of Value that time wasted is existence, while time used is life.

There are certain approaches to life which will benefit you more than others. If, for example, you follow the Ballance Corollary that you should lose as if you like it and win as if you were used to it, you will not only become more adept at coping on a day-to-day basis, but you will also fake out a lot of people.

Also, if you want to live a long time, it may behoove you to live as if you are ten years older than you really are. However, it is an unalterable fact that anytime you hear someone say: "Youth is a state of mind," you can be sure that he has a lot more state of mind than he has youth.

Life is a freeway and weekends are filling stations along the way. In addition, for those of you who are hardcore gamblers, life is like a game of bridge, and only a dummy puts all of his cards on the table. It is a Palsied Postulate that life *justifies* itself only by the amusement it gives, probably because of the fact that most lives are one long improvisation, mainly a protracted series of fantastic haphazards. It's a long process of getting increasingly tired, this game of life, and if it were lived backwards, from old age to youth, there'd be an awful lot more juvenile delinquency.

A person brings nothing into this world and takes nothing out of it; and considering the kind of world it is, he's extremely lucky to break even. That's because we all learn, ultimately, the Ballance Axiom that life is really a series of gradually reduced expectations.

So enjoy yourself more, as you wonder what's next. The thing that makes living fascinating is that life is seething with improbabilities. Just being alive is a daily celebration of yourself. Permit nothing but the best from yourself. Cherish every instant of time you're aboveground. Stay loose, keep your life uncomplicated, and always keep this in mind—to be clever, all you need to do is remember a phrase that nobody else has ever thought of.

If you're one of those people of whom it takes all kinds to make a world; if you are competitively incompetent, mentally adrift and reaching a crescendo of self-pity; if you have that respectful unobtrusiveness of one whose mission in life is to be ignored, I hereby promote you to Charter Member of the Comic Order of Men Born to be Deceived.

> *Never hold a grudge—just*
> *get even—for through revenge*
> *we learn to forgive.*

Laws and Gossip

I must first point out that there is a vast difference between putting your nose in other people's business and putting your heart in other people's problems. It is an unerring Ballance Law that gossip is the art of saying nothing in a way that leaves nothing unsaid. A Perfunctory Postulate is that gossip is a vice enjoyed vicariously. It is the sweet, often malicious, subtle satisfaction without the risk . . . as it uncovers a mother lode of malice.

Be realistic—a gossip always gives you the benefit of the dirt. Personally, I think that all vicious rumors should be fitted with heavy-duty girdles to keep them from spreading. Remember that it is foolish simply to repeat gossip. Be more creative—make some up.

Gossip is syndicated rumors, and the reasons people don't mind their own business is that they have no mind, in the first place and, in the second place, they have no business. So never tell anybody anything which they might, in turn, tell the wrong person. Remember Bill's Law of Loose Labia: Nothing is opened more by mistake than the mouth.

Let me now establish that involvement is essentially another word for meddling, and that gossip is primarily a process of forgiveness through vengeance. So if your day is full of malicious malquotations, don't be surprised. Remember Ballance's Inexorable Law of Inane Chatter: Gossip, like a vulture, prefers its meat rancid. As a corollary to that, a vicious rumor is as hard to *un*spread as spoiled butter.

Thanks to my enervating research, it is now a certified feminine fact that it is far easier for a woman to defend her virtue against men than her reputation against women. Which, incidentally, refers right back to Ballance's Law of Codified Rumormongering: People are not interested in anything unless it's none of their business. But if you persist, and want to skyrocket to the highest level of gossip achievement, remember Ballance's Law of Malevolent Muttering: It's not so much what you know that makes you a top-seeded gossip, it's whom you know it about that counts. If there's a sudden silence when you enter a room, it's never a good idea to ask what's cooking; they've probably just had *you* on the griddle.

Gossips are the *spies of life.* Some women clean house all morning so they can go out and spread dirt all afternoon. It is only world history that repeats itself. Your private history is repeated by the neighbors, who suck scandal like lollipops. Just watch some woman with an orchid face and a cactus tongue sitting there in an agony of suppressed information. She knows that women's gossip is the spark that sets off the explosion in the powder room. Her favorite indoor sport is attending hen parties, where everything is torn apart but the chicken. Her

If there's a sudden silence when you enter a room, it's never a good idea to ask what's cooking, they've probably had you *on the griddle.*

conversation is full of tatty little fragments of idle speculation and malicious malquotations. She says, "Girls [that's what women over 40 call each other], let's skip the facts and get down to the whispers." She then drops a name into the conversation and sits back to listen.

Next to dancing with a high-stepping strutter in stiletto-pointed shoes, nothing is more terrifying to a man than to observe the chilling antics of bored women obsessively engaged in planting daggers in the delicate backs of their best friends.

> *The reason a small town has more gossips than*
> *a city is this: It's more fun watching*
> *a game if you know the players . . . especially if*
> *their philosophy is, "If you can't say something*
> *good about a person, say it anyway* —somebody's
> bound to enjoy it."

Laws of the Heart

For thousands of years, there's been a half-baked theory that love is everything. Well, I'd like to clarify that. It's wrong. Success and the acquisition of wealth and power have always, and will always leave love quivering all alone at the post. This is known as Ballance's Law of Pari-Mutuel Passion. Nonetheless, some kinds of love are all-pervasive, like *self*-love, which is at least a lifelong romance. A few guidelines always help. Here they are, fresh from the recalibrated quill of your buddy Bill.

The Law of Loving Enzymes says that when you're in love, you need less food. All porkers take heed. When you're in love, your image of yourself improves and you don't gorge yourself so much. When you are desperately in love, you grow thin.

Never make love with strangers, unless you make love stranger than they do. This is Bill's Ships-Passing-in-the-Night Postulate. Man cannot live by misdemeanors and small romantic felonies alone, but in matters of the heart, a little sparkling larceny never hurt anyone.

In the battle of love, you should always retrieve your own wounded; never abandon them on the field of amour, lest one day you find your own heart at half-mast and your love in a sling.

Men—avoid prying into a girl's previous affairs. Never be jealous of the unalterable tangle of her romantic past. And, of course, never tell a girl that you're unworthy of her. Let that come later, as a surprise.

My Libidinous Law states that the weaker sex is really the stronger sex, because of the weakness of the stronger sex for the weaker sex. This only holds true if you don't confess to your new lover all those lecherous details of your hyperactive romantic past. Observe with caution: When a girl confesses to her lover all about her nimble past, the only thing he regrets is that he didn't know her sooner. An alternate, or variable constant corollary is this: Anything you tell someone you love, eventually will be used against you. Insecurity is the mother of confession.

When a man and a woman exchange searching looks with glowing eyes and wisps of steam curling out of their ears, it is known as Ballance's Law that at that very moment, they have reached an unspoken agreement and emotional history is about to be made. And as long as man is able to make love, it is an undeniable economic fact that diamond stocks will continue to rise.

But any grunthead can start a love affair. It takes finesse, delicate skill, to phase it out, to wind it down, to end it like a gentleman with no bitter tears and recriminations and without that irritating emotional macramé known as "strings." Personalities must be taken into sensitive and gentle consideration.

And remember, girls, how you apply your lipstick is not nearly as important as on whom for, indeed, my dear, *Love is Space and Time, measured by the Heart.*

Next area I shall descend sternly on is jealousy. By the power inherent in my vestments, I declaim Ballance's Law of Corrosive Jealousy: Nobody can take a girl away from a guy unless she *wants* to be taken. Whereas, a guy can be taken away from a girl any time he feels the urge, which is early and often. But jealous humanoids are always flint-hearted, because their ruling passion is pride, not love. Jealousy is the most corrosive and destructive of all emotions. It's a disease of the character, a soul-ravaging curse, a searing psychic flaw; it's the only vice that gives no pleasure.

> *The man who claims he can read women*
> *like a book can always be found*
> *browsing among the new editions.*

Laws of the Wallet

This brief, tightly woven outline should help you put certain essential economic factors into perspective. The cornerstones to my philosophy regarding cash are Ballance's Rule of Avarice, or Get It Now, and the contention that money cannot buy happiness, but it puts you in a great bargaining position. True, rich people have problems too. But paying bills isn't one of them.

Money can't buy friends, and that's a fact. But it is Ballance's Law of Low Overhead that if you have money, you can rent them. And of course you don't need money to get married, but a good diamond will cut into anything, especially a man's bank account.

Lack of money is the root of all evil—that's why I'm always in there rooting. Money may not be everything, but it's close. As for alimony, well it's a Ballance Poignant Proclamation that alimony is the money a woman gets for helping to make a mistake. As a subsidiary corollary to that throbbing observation, alimony is derived from single blessedness with double indemnity.

Money pulls even the most cohesive molecules apart. This is known as Ballance's Law of the Swollen Pecuniary Gland.

Its Fiscal Corollary: It's not the cost of the gift that counts, it's how much money was spent. 'Tis better to have loved and lost, but is it deductible?

Work and save and someday you'll have enough to divide with those who don't.

Sad is the person who has too much to live on and too little to live for, because we can always live on less when we have more to live for . . . and don't believe that till you're rich.

Unearned money can be a curse. Kids who grow up knowing they'll inherit a bundle or who know they'll always have a steady income without lifting a finger are likely to turn into human ciphers with no strong inner core. They've had nothing to pit themselves against, there have been no challenges, no opportunity to develop their will power and psychic strength. Through no fault of their own, they've been robbed of the joy of achievement, deprived of the exhilirating fun of accomplishment.

While I'm not a registered miser, I do have a passion for solvency, and it comes from having survived the Depression; that's why, today, I'm a heavy stockholder in Skinflint Savings and Loan, a corporate result of a recent merger between Misplaced Trust Company and The Absconders' and Defaulters' National Bank. Patrick Henry should come back today and see what taxation *with* representation is like. He'd agree with me in warning you about being a creditor. Character is the only thing on which anyone can safely lend money. All other things are subject to change. Only character withstands change, resists attack, and rises from defeat. As it is the only foundation for any lasting happiness, so is it the only security for a loan.

Because of my fiscal prudence, I've avoided the stock market; I have no faith in it. If I invested in mouthwash stock, for example, bad breath would suddenly become popular; if I bought AT&T, telepathy would be perfected.

> *Anyone who says that money cannot*
> *buy happiness has had very little*
> *experience with either one.*

Laws of General Behavior

Behavior comes in patterns. The pendulum swings from Nietzschean nihilism and drugs to frantic religious fervor and pseudosentiment. The opposite of psychedelic is nostalgic, just as the opposite of hallucinating is remembering. Thus, some get caught in between and psychiatrists thrive. It is written that a psychiatrist is a man who tells you things about yourself you already suspect, in words you don't understand, and at a price you can't afford. His game is psychiatry, which hinges on casting intellectual spells, reciting incantations, and finding parents guilty.

This is the age of the half-read page, of the instant hash and the headlong dash, where the night is bright with nerves uptight, then the jet-plane hop and the frantic stop. We are all role players, and you can always tell when a role player is well adjusted: His intake of pep pills outweighs his consumption of tranquilizers just enough to allow sufficient energy for daily trips to his shrink.

Everything is relative, and if you still don't know what relativity is, observe Ballance's Law: How long a minute is depends on which side of the bathroom door you happen to be on. I have a theory, soon to be collated into a Ballance Coaxial

Code, that television adds tremendously to the irrationality of the world, because television makes everything simpler or more dramatic or more immediate than it really is. And whatever you do, don't watch daytime television unless I happen to be on it. Any electrical appliance in your house, including your vacuum cleaner, offers more entertainment possibilities than daytime television.

Behaviorally, the worst part about having no judgment (watching daytime TV, for example), is that you never miss it. Which brings us to Ballance's Second Law of Unified Opposites: People who forget to turn off their car headlights always remember to lock the doors, with the keys inside. Still, it's better to be careful a thousand times than to be killed once. That's because the distance from here to eternity is one foot—on the accelerator.

It is written, citizens, that *survival* is *sustained achievement;* it is also written (with a Q-Tip dipped in Kool-Ade) that great respect for the truth is beneficial, if it is used frugally. That is because the only difference between virtue and vice is motive, and people who live in glass houses *don't* very much. It is also indiscreet, by the way, for a rat to gnaw at a tiger's tail; this is an ancient Oriental proverb I found written on the back of an old Chinese agency man, and it means that underlings are unwise when they claw at their overlords.

Always treat people fairly. When you break a promise, give another just as good. You've got to have sovereignty over yourself, after all. So never quarrel with your twin, either. If it weren't for him or her, you'd have two heads. And speaking of twins, beware of what you plant in your conscience for conscience is like a second self; if it's disturbed, you have to live with it; a troubled conscience is like being joined to an insane Siamese twin for the rest of your anguished life.

Observe Ballance's Absolute Optical Dictum: Glass walls do not a prism make.

Never waste time crying over spilt bygones. It is a Crumbling Corollary that after the ball is over, it's too late to swing the bat. And my mind of overweening superficiality just jostled me to point out rhythmically that it's always darkest before the dawn, so leave the light in the bathroom on. Remind yourself that too much of a good thing can be wonderful, but stop ricocheting into that center divider; remember Ballance's Caroming Corollary: Lane borders lane and there isn't much leeway in the home of the hip and the land of the freeway. Which reminds me: You cannot fool all of the people all the time, but freeway signs come mighty close.

Well, when something defies description, I say let it. Still, when you feel ready to give a terminal prognosis, remember Ballance's Iconoclastic Law: Bowling is a ball, peeling ears of corn is a shuck, and wearing clothes of the opposite sex is a drag. Remember not to be too broadminded. Ballance's Riparian Reflection states that minds, like streams, may be so broad that they are shallow.

I think that all gruntheads are also poor listeners. Take Ballance's Law of Acoustics for example: At a party, a talker raises the level of his voice in reflex response to an increase in the noise around him, but at the cost of intelligibility. Thus the talker puts things less accurately and he is, therefore, less accurately understood by his equally gruntbrained and garrulous listeners. It pays, in the long run, to avoid arguing anyway, especially with a fool. It's too difficult for the bystanders to know which is which.

However, if you do get into an argument with your lover, never let the sun set on it; buy a sunlamp and fight all night. The sooner you make new friends, after all, the sooner you'll have old ones, even though tension between people has a tendency to kill communication. But if you get in a bind, write it all down, because the one thing most of us can do better than anybody else is read our own handwriting.

Most behavior has some kind of deeper clue to subtle and hidden thoughts or actions. For example, if you drop a fork, it's a sign that company is coming. But if a fork is missing, it's a sign that company has already been there. Likewise, one picture window is worth a thousand words, especially to your neighbors. It is Ballance's Law of Unrequited Ignorance that no man

One picture window is worth a thousand words, especially to your neighbors.

looks in the closet unless he's stood there himself; I've hidden in so many closets, the moths know me by my first name.

I believe in courage, freedom of movement and expression, and the right to spontaneous response, as long as it doesn't harm anyone. But never underestimate the power of stupid people in large groups. Nothing is more terrifying than ignorance in action. It's a small world, but that's what they get for not having it Sanforized, and the only person who saves time is one who spends it well.

Incidentally, if your man is always late, remember Ballance's Law of Unpunctuality: Tardiness is always a disapproval or avoidance syndrome; your man doesn't really want to do whatever it is that he's late for, and he doesn't respect the value of your time, which is inexcusable rudeness. If all else fails, remember Ballance's Pythagorean Axiom: You can't teach an old dog new math.

Another area of concern is the behavioral work situation. It is a Ballance Law of Sodden Perspiration that you're really working for a living when you feel you'd rather be doing something else.

Equal pay for equal results, I always say, mostly because brilliance without discipline is like a syringe without vaccine, and discipline is what gets things done. It is a Piercing Postulate that one should never mistake intention to work for work already completed.

It's always better to feel remorse for what you've done than to feel regret for what you failed to do. Experience is a positive by-product, because even though training means learning the rules, experience means learning the exceptions. In addition, if you reveal your plans, it dissipates your desire to carry them out, so keep your cool and remember Ballance's Law of Upward Mobility: Do a little more each day than is expected of you, and very soon, more *will* be expected of you. And always keep in mind that it's far easier to get ahead if you were born with one.

Sometimes behavior can get mighty tricky. I don't happen to drink, for example, and sometimes it's awkward. If a man doesn't drink at all, he has the appearance of spying on others. So I always pretend I'm drinking heavily, and when I leave parties, staggering and flailing about like a moth caught in a beam of light, I try to throw up on the hostess to confirm my conviviality. My favorite spectator sport is watching dt's.

Difficulties can also arise in specialized occupations. Take prostitution, for example. Prostitution, like other professions, constitutes a conspiracy against the public, but unlike other professionals, prostitutes make no false claims for themselves, and in the course of a long history they have always imparted much pleasure, which is more than lawyers can say . . . except when they haughtily draw up their briefs and observe that venereal disease is nothing to clap about.

It is written that everyone should keep someone else's diary, and I can't for the life of me figure out why, unless it would be a loose life document. It reminds me of Ballance's Mathematical Maze: A line perpendicular to one of two parallel lines is perpendicular to the other line too, for a good line is the shortest distance between two dates. But once again, be careful. Never judge a dentist by the size of his drill and avoid buying on time: Of all the ills through which man squirms, the hardest one is easy terms.

Speaking of easy, Ballance's Law of Intermittent Vacations just leaped into my head: Comfort is the happiness of the indolent, whereas pleasure is the comfort of the unhappy. Let that penetrate your crenellated cranium as you admit that the only true aphrodisiac is variety, and the only way to avoid being a wallflower is to get rid of that pot.

I shall wind up this churlish chapter by emphasizing that a pedestrian may have the right of way, but a car has more momentum. Ergo, if you have a dull day, it's your own fault. Exuberance is highly contagious so, if you're on the phone, don't hesitate to exube especially if you are talking to your lover; because that which we give a beloved, we give without relinquishing; and never overanalyze your love affair; analyzing an affair is like dissecting a frog—when you pluck it apart you find out what it's made of, but the subject is killed in the process.

Until next we meet, remember that the only setback that is final is the one that gets you embalmed and buried. So at your first reverse, don't throw yourself into the rubbish barrel; behavior becomes a moot point once you're dead. But don't dwell on it, don't brood and ponder, just remember Ballance's Credo for Morticians: Rigor mortis is not contagious, and the most pleasant surprise for any of us has got to be reincarnation.

Watch that nicotine intake and remember Ballance's Diagnostic Digression: Piano keys are white because elephants don't smoke.

Ballance Laws of Science and Research

BB Axiom: do not merely *believe* in miracles—*rely* on them.

BB Basic Principle and Ultimate Precept: by definition, when you are investigating the Unknown, you do not know what you will find, nor will you understand what you have found, when that thrilling moment arrives.

BB Compensation Corollary: any experiment may be considered a success if no more than 50 percent of the observed measurements must be hastily discarded to correspond with established fustian theory.

BB Futility Factor: no experiment is ever a complete failure, inasmuch as a carefully written document about it can serve admirably as a publish-or-perish striving for academic tenure.

BB Effect: those items most urgently needed are inversely available to the degree of the urgency of the need; i.e., in any pile of papers, when search is begun at the top the sought-after document will always be found at the bottom.

BB Law of the Perversity of Inanimate Objects: any inanimate object, regardless of its composition or configuration, may be expected to perform at any unpredictable time in a totally unexpected manner for reasons that are either totally obscure and/or illogical.

BB Law of Proper Graphing: first draw the curves, then plot the data.

BB Coefficient Code: the probability of a given event occurring is inversely proportional to its desirability.

BB Five-Thumb Postulate: experience varies directly with the amount of equipment irrevocably ruined by clumsy assistants who have encumbered you with their help.

BB Corollary: if anything can go wrong, it will; i.e., if you drop a piece of toast on an expensive carpet, it will always land butter-side down.

BB Constant: that quantity which, when multiplied X-times, is divided into, added to, subtracted from, or taken to the power of the answer you got, yields readily to the answer in the back of your book.

BB Spare Parts Permutation: the accessibility, during recovery of small parts which fall from the workbench (known as Spacelab Syndrome), varies directly with the size of the part, and inversely with its importance to the completion of the project underway.

BB Principle of Methodical Order and Random Variables: those supplies necessary for yesterday's experiment must be ordered no later than by noon tomorrow with countless eager ergs of resourceful prescient energy.

BB Stern Rules of Experimental Procedure: before your meticulous beginning of any project, you must be resigned to one significant fact—that anything that can go wrong will go wrong, and that when it goes wrong, it all goes wrong at the same time; hence, you have but one course: Give yourself a way out, known as Ballance's Law of Extrication, namely the Cosmic Copout: You may recall Ballance's Constant, a multiplier of the Zero Order Term, characterized by changing the Universe to fit the Equation. The Ballance Sub-Factor allows you to change (imperceptibly) the equation to fit the Universe; this is sometimes known among the irreverent as the Soothing Factor. Mathematically similar to the Damping Factor, it has the characteristic of dropping the entire subject under examination to Ground Zero importance and gives your experiment chemically pure weightlessness. Crucial, of course, is the overwhelming necessity for you to avoid building any mechanism *simply* if a way can be found to make it complex and . . . well, wonderful.

Man is only the ancestor of the computer, and his sole role is to develop the circuits that will take his place, for science is the eternal quest for knowledge that has brought man to the point where he is now creating his own successor.

Chapter Two
Love

Passionate Love

When a love affair is too intense, it is doomed from the start—it burns itself out. But the main enemy of love is the passage of time. Time is a self-devouring volcano, and as for unrequited love, forget it. What's gone is gone, and you might as well let it be woven into the emotional fabric of years gone by. Don't look back; there isn't time, and time is the most valuable thing in life. Time is the only irreplaceable commodity—whereas love can grow again. When love for one particular individual is gone, it's gone forever, sunk in the receding past, so learn to let go. Remember Ballance's Law of Emotional Resurrection: You cannot discover new oceans unless you have courage to lose sight of the shore.

Passionate love is a frenzy of imagination. A young girl I know is in love with a struggling, fate-buffeted, hard-hat construction worker. She's convinced that he learned to kiss like that by catching hot rivets in his mouth.

I believe, however, that passionate, devouring love can exist only between strangers. The rich, tranquil love of husband and wife is something different. It is purer but less intense, saner but less exciting. It is friendship, whereas the other is domination and surrender. Married love can strengthen and give life. Passionate, consuming love is violent and terminal; I believe it yearns to end in emotional death. Wonder and danger are the earliest sensations of a passionate love. The lover sees the woman, this particular woman, as though she belonged to a different world from his own. She will, if she is receptive, admit him to that magical world, but it may be perilous for him, and it may change his whole nature. It is impossible for him to tell; all he knows is that he must follow her when she takes his eager, perspiring hand. Passionate desire in a man happens first; it's the woman who transforms it into enduring love. Yet passionate love is never eradicated from the memory, even when the heart has become . . . well, realistic under the pitiless beat of time and change.

But let me admonish you with Ballance's Law of Emotional Clout, which states that when you're deeply in love, you give someone else too much emotional leverage on your destiny. When you *give* yourself entirely, you're in someone else's captivating clench. Conversely, when you are *not* involved, you are liberated from thralldom, from emotional bondage; you are no longer tethered to painful memories.

A reputation once broken may
possibly be repaired, but the
world will always keep its eye
on the spot where the crack appeared.

Consuming and Contented Love

The first and most important thing to remember is that love is every bit as nice as "The Bill Ballance Show": You can't explain its hold on you, but after awhile you accept it, and reveal it to your friends. But whether he's a performer or not, it is important for a man to realize that he has a terrific edge in life when he is *not* in love. *When a man is in love or in debt, someone else has the advantage.* The only thing that I'm in love with, by the way, is the sound of my own voice; that's why I always wear headphones, even when I'm not broadcasting.

Love is a feeling that has the incredible power of making you believe what you would normally treat with deep suspicion. It is a mutual admiration society made up of two members; of these, the one whose love is the least intense is always in control.

Intense love always makes people nervous. It's like being invited to a formal party where you're not quite sure if your table manners are correct.

To a woman, love is life, but to a man love is the joy of life. Misfortune in love will bruise the heart of a man, but it ruins the life òf a woman and wrecks her happiness. It is really a profound psychological question, whether a woman can truly love twice in her life. My work is—and always has been—my first love, which gives me an advantage when those hammer strokes of fate pummel my head and heart; after years in the amatory arena, I decided it's *performing* first, *loving* second, and a blending of both as often as possible. I love my work (broadcasting) in a careful, controlled manner, however, in the way a man loves a woman he doesn't quite trust.

The true measure of love is what you're willing to give up for it, and the self-knowledge that just because you've enjoyed hugging and kissing someone for ten years doesn't mean it'll last forever. Be grateful it lasted as long as it did, and don't whimper for amnesty when it's over. Cowards cringe for clemency.

Love means never having to ask, "How was it?" Love is when

life is at its most vibrant intensity—which you can easily detect, because where love is, no one can hide it for long, and where love is not, none can simulate it. Love is the most complete response of which a human being is capable.

Ah, how quickly love flowers in the hearts of the young, inexperienced, and foolish—brimming with tumescent temerity. When those hormones are flushing through your veins like Peruvian nettles, you're the enchanted victim of romantic hallucination, but no harm will be done if you remember Ballance's Stark Reality Rule, namely that love is the *ideal* thing; marriage is the *real* thing. Confusion of the real with the ideal never goes unpunished. Love must be built on truth, not on dreams, and the knowledge of what we recognize ourselves to be, rather than on what we think it is fashionable to be.

Love is a holiday that can be celebrated every day, but love *never* survives a sense of captivity, so if you feel captured, watch with dismay the dilution of your love and its gradual evaporation.

Women who must schedule their love, threshing around only at certain hours of the day (Prime-Time Passion) have forgotten that lovemaking must be spontaneous; you can't really regulate that estrogen churning through your amorous aorta, and to do so will turn you prematurely blonde.

Love affairs are like tuning forks: You have to sound them often to keep your life up to pitch. And if yours is a one-sided affair, don't brood over it, because it is written, "The love that lasts the longest is the love that's never returned."

At its best, love is concern and commitment in its ultimate dimension; it turns one person into two, and two into one, and, although you can't buy love, you can buy something that looks and acts like love. It is a Ballance axiom to love thy neighbor, but don't get caught.

Love is by its nature narcissistic. It comes from the recognition of oneself in another, but it is not egoistic or possessive and cannot be experienced between men and women when women are not allowed autonomy. Most lovers in our society are merely playing out an exercise in mutual psychological dependence. Their aim is not to love one another but to become, each to the other, *indispensable.* Thus our main thrust is love, even though love is the ultimate vulnerability.

When you're in love, the whole world's organic. I know one girl, for example, who's so loving and gentle she won't even eat a Popsicle. Not because it isn't organic, but because she's afraid of hurting the poor little thing with her teeth.

Love is the tie that binds which matrimony buckles together, because a man reserves his greatest and deepest love, not for the woman in whose company he finds himself electrified and galvanized by passion, but for the woman in whose company he feels relaxed and tenderly drowsy. Love's gift is the courage to confide; but don't confide too much. Anything intensely intimate you tell a loved one will eventually be used against you. I've said that before in this glorious book, but I want to reemphasize it.

No woman ever falls in love with a man unless she has a better opinion of him than he deserves, which gives most men a choice: They can love their women or they can understand them. I happen to have an obssessive love for all females from infancy until that depressing day they're cramming for their finals.

True love is enduring, but it is also fragile. When held tightly, true love warms the soul, but when held too tightly, it breaks like a brittle light bulb. But the biggest mistake made by lovers is to regard it as a game in which there are prescribed moves and counter-moves. Actually, love is instinctive, requiring not thought nor intellectual agonizing, but instinct. The first instinct is a desire to give, rather than take, and most men flunk the first test.

Perfect love means to love the one through whom one can easily become unhappy, even though this viewpoint could conceivably reduce the idea of love to a dirty trick nature played on us to achieve certain continuation of the species.

An ultra-clever girl, who has a dozen lovers, might be an exception, but only if she is able to multiply her love without dividing its worth.

Romance is when a woman has woman-power over a man, and to the delight of both of them, becomes more important to him than other things. That's why love is like life insurance; the older you get, the more it costs. This is a tender but taut parable for everyone who has overtrained for the tag-game match of love.

Love is space and time, measured by the heart.

Love never remains constant, as we all play our roles in the ancient emotional comedy of advance and retreat. It pays to watch your step, though, and be especially careful about your commitments: Love is never having to say you're (a) ruptured; (b) swaybacked; (c) eviscerated; or (d) embalmed.

Love between unequals can never succeed, even though modern love affairs are like business agreements; no frills, no flowers, no time wasted on elaborate compliments, verses, or lengthy seductions, no complications, and no scenes, please. In this hectic, high-pressure age, girls are expected to accelerate their passions to save time for themselves and their lovers. It's as if they're emotionally double-parked.

Love takes time; to court and love someone in a satisfactory manner is a game with many time-consuming phases. People haven't stopped making love any more than they've stopped eating. But to extend the surprisingly apt parallel joys of gourmethood, less time is devoted to both preparation and savoring. And never mind that old saw about spices; the only true aphrodisiac is variety.

Personally, it's taken me a lifetime to decide always to make up my own mind about women; what's the good of other people's opinions? Animals never consult each other about other animals; they look and sniff, touch and listen. Those are the only tests that really matter in love and hate and everything in between.

The mistake people make about love is trying to find it in others without finding it first in themselves. We are all anxious to fall in love, and be fallen-in-love with, because it is a waste of life to move through space and time without love. Take care to avoid mistaking habit for love (romantic ritual), and remember that when love strikes like lightning, the thunder can last a lifetime.

Love grows out of a mutual need and responsiveness, a sharing of intense desire and pleasure. He who lives to love today will love to live another day; for indeed love makes time pass, and time makes love pass. And a man always falls in love with the woman who asks the kind of questions he can answer brilliantly.

In love, no man begins to be serious until he begins to act ridiculous.

Love is a condition that makes your head swim and your heart sink, and if you could harness the energies of love, you could, for the second time, discover fire. Love is the strongest motivation in life, followed by a craving for communication, and that's why I tell you about it on my shows all the time. But I'm beginning to wonder—if all the world loves a lover, how come so many husbands are mad at me?

Under the most rewarding circumstances, love is the accurate estimate and supply of another's needs, which are then cherished. Some lovers are possessors, and some are the possessed, while others are merely placid or deeply devious. This is right if the emotional anarchy is shared and neither person is used simply as the other's victim.

Love should be an act of will, of impassionated patience; it should be flexible, cunning, constant. Love should provide insulation against the fire or frost of shifting moods. This is because we are born dehydrated, mortal and ordinary, until love plumps us up, dilates the eyes, puts a glow on the skin, and helps us see in another person a particular kind of niftiness.

This eternal game of love began in prehistoric times and is destined to continue until we're all vaporized in a nuclear mist. In matters of romance, most girls hate a quitter, and they don't care much for a beginner, either, in this, the ultimate hustle.

Love knows no honor; people in love do things that they never thought they'd do and that they've always despised other people for doing. These same people violate not only their own scruples, but their own style. What a man won't do for money he *will* do for a woman. People rarely make a declaration of love without expecting a response, and a man can love a woman even though she doesn't excite him anymore—but if love were a nonrenewable commodity, we'd all be in trouble. Fortunately, we can always fall in love again, although I, personally, haven't been in love for hours.

It is important to realize that love is a multifarious agitation that makes a man ripe for torment and ready for cuddly conciliation. Although soundless when it arrives, it's mighty noisy when it leaves. Sometimes ulterior motives are involved, like the time I really felt it was lasting love for me, when I held her in my arms and said I was hers, body and soul, but she wanted to know what else I had to offer, something perhaps a trifle more *tangible.*

Love involves a good deal of faith; faith in the sense of allowing yourself to be vulnerable and open to disappointment. You love someone because of what he or she is, not because of what he or she does or doesn't do to prove sincere love. There are no conditions and no demands among considerate lovers, except the ones they impose upon themselves individually.

Love looks forward, and hate looks back, while jealous anxiety has eyes all over its head.

A teenage couple can live on love, provided it's that of the bride's father, and a middle-aged man can fall in love and be perfectly contented, provided he doesn't discover that he was looking through the wrong half of his bifocals. Love just makes the world go round like a termite in a yo-yo—it is oceans of emotions surrounded by an expanse of expense. But pity the woman who marries for life and then finds out that he doesn't have any.

Love begins when another person's welfare becomes more important than your own, and even though heredity may determine the color of your eyes, love is what brightens them up. The difference between friendship and love has to do with the relative position of the individuals involved: Friendship is an exchange between equals, but love an abject relationship between tyrants and slaves, and the one who loves the least is the tyrant in command of the slave. Remember—when you're lonesome for love, you're ripe for trouble.

Men prefer to make a love affair an interlude, while women yearn to make it a career. Despite the fact that love is the intense concentration of two people on one another, it is an absolute fiscal fact that any girl whose love a man can buy will eventually be bought from him.

You always grow out of a first love, but you never get over it. It is fortunate that love at first sight enables us to make our biggest mistakes while we're young. Still, one of the fascinating things about being in love is the way two people develop prejudices, secret meanings of code-words and gestures, and a private vocabulary, so that they can exchange intimate, amused glances, and feel just a shade superior to all outsiders.

Men always want to be a woman's first love, while women have a more subtle instinct: What a woman likes is to be a man's last romance. But like all other violent excitements, love emphasizes not only what is best, but what is worst in men's characters. Just as some men are malicious and brawling when they drink, so are they moody and jealous and demanding when they're in love. The emotions, for men as well as for women, are no respecters of the niceties and proprieties of life. The chief effect of love is to drive a man half crazy, while the chief effect of marriage is to finish the job.

Love is parsley on the entertainment of life, especially when people can surge ecstatically into each other's arms gazing at each other with steaming eyes, with little wisps of passionate smoke curling out of their ears.

Love is like a flame; a little oil makes it burn much brighter.

Some women are difficult to please, though, like a dollbaby I know who said to me: "Bill, all I want is a nice guy to love me and understand me. Now, I ask you, is that too much to expect from a millionaire?" That same delightful girl, incidentally, has never been in love, but she has been in a lot of cars.

Quarreling lovers avoid each other at parties like enemy diplomats. Have you ever noticed how they practice together-apartness? Or apart-togetherness? But when married couples quarrel, the wife cunningly strikes back at her husband by either undressing for bed in the bathroom, or by undressing in front of him *with her back turned.* This maneuver is subtle rejection and always infuriates the male.

Some women have an irresistible love technique: They begin by resisting a man's advances, and then they finish by blocking his retreat.

Love is the need to escape oneself, but if you and your lover are temporarily apart, don't worry about it. Remember, the same wind that snuffs out a candle can also kindle a forest fire. Thus, where absence kills a shallow love, absence fans a deep love.

Love is the effort a man makes to be satisfied with only one woman; it is a temporary insanity curable by marriage. Love is a season pass on that emotional shuttlecraft between heaven and hell.

Life is a terrifying unknown, redeemed by man's two contradicting passions: To establish order, and then to risk that order through acts of love.

You cannot build a love nest with another man's bird, which is proof positive that love quickens all senses but the common. So, men, before you fall in love with a pair of bright eyes make sure it isn't the sun shining through a hole in the back of her head that makes them bright. Yes, I've said that before, but I like the ring of it.

Maintaining the tension of a love affair gives us a curious satisfaction, even though I believe most men should be more pragmatic in their amorous approaches. If you're a businessman, you know that true love is based upon trust . . . funds. You should say to a girl: "Well, lady, we each have something the other wants, and that is a good solid basis for a bargain which could be mutually beneficial. So it's barter time, and let's have no restraint of trade. I may even grow to love you like my own cash and blood."

We carnivorous bipeds are always thirsting for love, forgetting that *too much dependence* on one another for emotional satisfaction always breeds hostility.

Love is built up gradually through contacts of the soul and interplay of personalities. When you are living with someone you really love, you are in a blissful state of reciprocal contribution, based on mutual knowledge of one another. Love is like a chemical reaction for which we have no formula; beware the immolative nature of a combustible relationship lest you find yourself sadly sifting the ashes of a burnt-out passion.

Love contributes to an unstable state of mind when two people are convinced that they think as much of each other as they think of themselves, for, though love has many dimensions, it can never survive mistrust; and mistrust is inevitable, because no two people ever loved each other with equal intensity.

Never vow perpetual devotion, because everything is transitory and, likewise, think carefully before you say you hate something, because hate implies as much attraction as love, even though it is the attraction of destruction.

You want to know the real reason why lovers never get bored? It's because they're always talking about themselves. And they joyfully recognize that at least making love still allows for human enterprise and imagination.

Love is like eating mushrooms: You don't know whether it's the real thing until it's too late. Love is also like potato salad: When you share it with someone, it's a picnic. Love starts when she sinks into your arms, and ends with her arms in the sink. Still, nothing is more annoying to a man than to hear a girl he's been having *fun* with suddenly tell him she can't live without him.

Real love makes you feel as if you've been dropped down a well; it makes everything wonderful, while hate, on the other hand, concentrates on the thing hated.

If we men were really the lovers we thought we were, you women wouldn't have time for anything else. So men, remember, when you fish for love, bait with your heart, not your brain. Otherwise you might wind up in a neurotic love affair, stitched forever to someone with those steel cables of fear and emotional need.

When a man is really in love, everything looks better, except

If we men were really the lovers we thought we were, you women wouldn't have time for anything else.

other women, but the only way to live on love is to own a drive-in movie. A romance is a love affair in which it takes two to make a quarrel and three to make it interesting, though if you want to know a sure way to tell if you and your girl are really in love, just see if you're willing to sit there and listen to her describe another woman's dress in detail, after which she must be willing to submit to your descriptive rehash of an entire ball game.

I have another tormenting truism, from the immortal quill of your admirer, Bill: Never overdo self-sacrifice; if you begin by sacrificing yourself to those you love, you will end by hating those to whom you have sacrificed yourself.

If you have love, it doesn't matter what you don't have, and if you don't have love, it doesn't matter what you do have. Just don't believe that until you have enough self-confidence to tell the world to kiss off.

The magic of first love is the ignorance that it can ever end.

Make sure, if you do take that plunge off the wharf of sanity, that you aren't simply infatuated. Here's how to tell: Love creates vitality, whereas infatuation only produces inertia. The best way for couples to distinguish between the two is by asking themselves if their mutual feeling turns them inward upon themselves, or outward upon the world.

Love is the only disease that those who don't have are trying to get; it has no basis in logic, and you can't feel it or see it walk in, but you really know when it walks out.

> *The inner braces of your heart*
> *must be equal to the outer pressures*
> *of life's circumstances.*

Jealousy

Jealousy is the only vice that gives no pleasure, so let's not dwell on it; it is the world's most useless, negative emotion. Jealousy is desperate and degrading; it's when you ask more questions but believe fewer answers. You are riding on the rim of Misery.

Jealousy is not proof of affection. On the contrary, jealous people are usually hard-hearted, for pride is their ruling passion, not love. They have a badly-shriveled character.

Jealousy is caused by a combination of basic emotions, among them the desire for love and attention, as well as the fear of losing that love—a dismal dread caused by a lack of self-confidence. Jealousy seizes humans who have a profound need for love, but who also have a deep-seated fear of betrayal.

Jealousy is a state of mind in which a human being watches coldly for clues of dissatisfaction, for hints of lies, and for hesitations in communication. Jealousy is a sad, pathetic state of affairs, and the most corrosive human emotion. Let's all give it a resounding "Booooooo!"

Jealousy is peering suspiciously
at someone through an imaginary keyhole.

Deterioration and Acrimonious Deviations

Ballance's Mystical Principle states that love slowly runs out, like the sand sifting through an egg timer. It is to your benefit to watch out for any love affair whose disintegration leaves a badly frayed ego and defoliated spirits. Those abrasive, lingering humiliations are not good for your tousled head. So be hyperalert to amorous attrition and emotional erosion as you poke through the romantic rubble of your anguished life.

Most all destructiveness stems from lack of love, or a general let-down from the initial bliss; you undergo the usual process of first the fever, then the rash. Love is like a coin after years of abrasive use, it gets worn and defaced and the inscription on it becomes illegible because the coin needs to be reminted. The love affair thus simply evolves into a series of diminishing expectations.

A woman unpursued is grim to see, for Hell hath no fury like a woman hunting for a new lover. If she was ensnared by a hopeless and twisted passion for some unreceptive swine, she must drop him and consider herself well out of it. If someone is blunting her will to live by causing a chronic drain on her emotional powers, she must step aside as gracefully as she can and not put it off until everything goes sour, like a mildewing washcloth; she must end it now, for there is no rage like the rage of the lawyer of a woman scorned.

Men, I offer you a harsh fact: Of all of life's emotional encumbrances, the most awkward is a woman we have ceased to love. Once a woman gives you her heart, it's hard to get rid of the rest of her. My experience has taught me that all love affairs end in tragedy; your temporary happiness is always snatched away, either by one lover engulfing the other, or by the onset of emotional atrophy. Men and women should remain together only as long as they love each other, and not a minute longer. And men, have you ever noticed that the most *punctual* woman you know is a woman you have ceased to care for?

Every relationship between two people of either sex starts going bad if one person is more successful than the other; there has to be an import-export quality to friendships. One exports what the other needs, and vice versa. When the balance of payments is disturbed, there is a falling out. Then a friend in need is a Pest indeed.

Dependency on friendship is something else that people should grow out of. If individuals continue to develop psycho-logically throughout their lives, whether as members of a marital unit or not, their need for friendship becomes progressively less. I don't mean that people don't continue to have friends, just that they don't feel a dependent need for them. Why not? Well, in a way, neurotic friendship is for ignorant beginners in life; it is for those who are not grown up, who have to be like everyone else, who have to be surrounded by people who love them. The price paid is conformity to a cluster of dreary, dull, unquestioned beliefs.

It is always difficult to phase out a friendship or a love affair without hurt feelings and bitter recriminations, along with rebuttal threats of vengeance. As you saunter over the horizon, the best thing to say is, "It's been more than somewhat."

Some women are like Saran Wrap—transparent, but hard to remove once you get wrapped up in them. If it's a serious affair, or once was, the end is always full of gentle melancholy, and your soul seems to have stopped dead, drained of all vitality.

If, however, you're not really in love, the possible pain you could cause your love-partner at this time must be weighed against the incalculable pain that would be continuously compounded in an unloving marriage. So, the best thing to do is to *let go,* because when love is gone, it's gone forever, sunk in your rapidly receding personal history.

All a love affair has to do is fade in the mind and heart of *one* participant, and suddenly the other person senses that something is wrong, and, instead, of projecting tender love, that person projects agonized anxious intensity, pleading: "Please don't leave me." But by then it's always too late. Reconciliations never work because human relationships are too fragile. You cannot reweave a cobweb.

If your former love nest has disintegrated into a storm center of screams, hysteria, lamentations, and counterthrusts, don't fight it; all love affairs must be allowed to run their natural course, and the natural course of all love affairs is this: Passion, Consummation, Contentment, Boredom, and Betrayal.

For you men, it would be wise to take note of a certain scary transformation in a woman when she decides to take a vindictive approach, when her tenderness turns to stone. Feminine

Some women are like Saran Wrap—transparent, but hard to remove once you get wrapped up in them.

reactions are intensely violent, and as soon as a woman's love for a man ceases, ruthlessness takes its place. Nothing can recall her vanished feelings and the efforts to do so, no matter how delicate and tenderly sincere, will only result in her icy snubs. In those eyes which yesterday flowed with surrender, there will be a savage stare, and from those lips which used to whisper undying devotion, calculated abuse will pour. You're lucky she doesn't pinch your cheek with a pair of pliers and jam a knee into your sweetbreads.

There is something sinister in this metamorphosis, something which suggests a ferocious cruelty and egoism lurking beneath that alabaster surface. In this situation, there are no such words as "pity" or "compassion," there is only her overwhelming desire to escape by scratching and tearing. Hate lies nearer to love in a woman's soul than in a man's soul, and it flowers with terrifying speed. Either boredom or misery can alter her personality with devastating results, and if she can injure and insult the man she so recently adored it produces a hot satisfaction in her blood. She is delighted. So, you guys, if you find yourselves confronted with this type of woman, be forewarned, and flee the scene.

Finally, when you lose someone you really love, you always feel that the loss is total, irreparable, and absolute; but if you'll just be patient with yourself you'll find that it's never true. I know. I've been down that road many times and can give directions.

Good breeding is that
splendid quality that
enables a person to wait
in well-mannered silence
while an oafish loudmouth
gets the service.

The Hypothetical Resurrection

Face it, lovers, an affair that is over can be *resumed,* but it can never be *revived.* Ah, those reconciliations; the complicated, apprehensive reweaving of two lives, with its hesitancies, its faint alarms, its doubts, its rediscoveries of mutual enjoyment while locked in mortal emotional combat. Reconciliations *never* really work out because they're based on pretense, on reciprocal deceit, on the false premise that two human beings really can forget the psychic damage they've done to each other.

Reconciliations are self-destructive; they're like a tennis match in hell with nobody missing the ball; it's a desperate situation which is doomed from the start. After a tortured love affair between two insecure people the exaltation and despair, mutual threats of romantic reprisal and defiant accusation can only lead to unhappiness. Everything becomes laced with undertones of violent passion and seething jealousy, with both man and woman unwilling to face the inevitability of a messy disentanglement. When you've battled ceaselessly and then sought help through counseling or psychotherapy, you return home and function under an armed truce, a sort of nonaggression pact. You weigh each other's words and inflections, you watch each other's gestures, you listen for significant pauses, you anticipate slights. Things can never be the same again, so grow up and face the fact that reconciliations never really work; you cannot reheat an old soufflé. You'll end up a study in dejection and go spiraling through life in an attitude of cowed resignation.

Chapter Three
Marriage *or* Bill Ballance's
Bursts of Insight

As one of the walking wounded from the Battle of Marriage, a colorfully scarred veteran of two protracted matrimonial wars, I feel incredibly well equipped to deal with this stifling human experiment.

That's right. Twice I was dipped in honey and spreadeagled on the anthill of marriage. For fifteen years, I wore my POW (Prisoner of Wedlock) parka around the house, and I've really paid my dues; I was subdivided twice financially.

Both my marriages started off as warm and meaningful tactility encounters; but then that great fermenting process set in, whereby love ripened into vengeance and my wives left me, in a fit of good taste. Of course, one of the times I committed matrimony, I don't even think I said "I do"; I suspect that her mother was a ventriloquist. Anyway, I knew that particular marriage was doomed from the start when she demanded separate bedrooms—on our honeymoon.

A few poignant memories remain, however, like the time I was rummaging around in my garage and found a piece of our wedding cake. It was all dry and crumbly and falling apart—a perfect allegory of the disaster it commemorated. She was the wife who tended to hit me over the head with her Chihuahua.

The other wife was a perfect housekeeper. All our dishes were shining and spotless—but I did get a little weary of eating out of pans.

I dated many girls before (and during) my marriages, but at least I didn't make the mistake that so many guys do. I did not marry my first love, and it's just as well because my first love was a certain coaster wagon in Peoria, Illinois.

Except for an occasional sharp clash, my marriages were one long nightmare; of course, being a performer, the main thing I didn't like about marriage was that it took my mind off myself.

And I don't like to be restricted to just one girl, either; as a lover, I'm inclined to be a general practitioner, not a specialist. What I'm looking for—my dream woman—is a slender creature between 21 and 35 who is hyperbright, with a great sense of humor and is raunchily affectionate (without being adhesive) twenty-four hours a day. She must be petite and portable and remarkable for her alertness to command. She must also have had her appendix out, she must own at least one pair of stout, no-nonsense walking shoes (sensible hiking oxfords accepted), one good warm coat suitable for any occasion, and she must have at least five good serviceable teeth, preferably in front.

Now that your peals of laughter have subsided, let me assure you that I don't react well to the confinement of marriage, that emotional straitjacket, because I need, in fact I thrive, on the freedom *to love, not the obligation.*

Marriage, to me, was suffocating—it was fifteen years of wedded atrophy. I like to prowl alone in the cool of the evening; I like to roam unencumbered and return to my fringy, dingy digs at Truculent Manor whenever I feel like it. I have a free-lance heart and refuse to be restricted for life to just one lovely creature. There are so many beautiful women, and so little time—and making love is, after all, the most exhilirating body-contact sport known to man, and it thrives on enterprise, imagination, and romantic resourcefulness.

So I'll spend the second half of my life bounding through boudoirs in a high, senile prance—winnowing the goats from the

gazelles—as I gather material for my next best seller: How to Court a Woman You Don't Really Want to Marry.
   OK, we're off in a cloud of heifer dust!

Marriage Is . . .

Face it, chums, marriage is the world's most expensive way of getting your laundry done free. . . . The only time it's a 50-50 proposition is when you both get married at that age (or when you're half drunk and she's half sober).

   I think marriage is just like a lottery, except for one thing: in a lottery, when you lose you can tear up your ticket.

   The devastating lack of discretion that creates a marriage situation is like boxing . . . the preliminaries are always better than the main event. Love is a fever that marriage puts to bed and cures, a feast at which the hors d'oeuvres are better than the entree, and that wedding night is the appetizer for a long, dull banquet.

   Listen guys, when you marry that artful hussy you're in a business in which you are forced to take your boss along on vacation. And taking a wife along on vacation is like going on an off-season hunting trip with the game warden.

   Really now, in a split second of solemnity, isn't marriage carrying love a little too far? We have before us a litany of gloom, a romance in which the hero gets killed in the first chapter.

   Why marry? Instead, take a nubile maiden with you on a magic-lantern lecture tour of those stucco horrors, our nation's crummiest, greediest wedding chapels. Look at it this way, marriage is nature's way of keeping men from fighting with strangers, or—even more terrifying—a woman's way of calling the meeting to order.

Incidentally, it is known as Ballance's Law that scoring is a game finally called on account of marriage.

I have also noticed that a married couple often becomes like a pair of scissors . . . joined so that they can't be separated, often moving in opposite directions, and yet cutting up anyone who tries to come between them. And you can always tell how long a couple has been married by the distance separating them when they're out for a stroll—that is, how far ahead of her he walks.

My own experience has verified that marriage is like a card game . . . it makes a lot of difference what kind of hand you're holding; and since prehistoric times, trumps have changed from clubs to diamonds.

I can also prove conclusively that marriage is what gives a man a new lease on life, but at double the rent.

But sharing is wonderful, especially when you admit you're wrong 50 percent of the time, and she admits she's right the other 50 percent. Most of the time marriage is a mutual partnership in which the husband is mute; it's a state of antagonistic cooperation.

Beneath a thin veneer of affability, men, lurks a feminist plot to add to a man's responsibilities and subtract from his rights. A disaster to many a courtship, marriage is like sitting in a steaming bathtub . . . once you get used to it, it's not so hot.

When an emotionally defoliated male marries, he accepts romantic blackmail and voluntarily surrenders his freedom of action and independence of thought. He soon learns that marriage simplifies life but complicates living.

Marriage is often the result of predatory passion, and partly the desire for property, which is a subdivision of the craving for power. To the average woman, a husband is highly valuable property. So, to the average man, is a wife. No other domestic animal is so useful, or so greatly gratifies the vanity of the owner. Thus, marriage is like woolen jockey shorts; warm, but binding.

As my acerbic insight would have it, marriage is a case of two people agreeing to change each other's habits. Marriage is therefore marvelous . . . it teaches a man loyalty, tolerance, patience, understanding, perseverance, and a lot of other things he wouldn't need if he'd stayed single.

Marriage—that tormented rest period between romances—is actually a raffle in which the winner draws alimony as a result of a combination of ghastly and monumental misunderstandings due to total togetherness.

The blessed state of community property, as I have come to know it, is a cage . . . the birds outside try desperately to get in, and those inside try desperately to get out. Thus, marriage is like a midnight phone call . . . you get a ring, and then you wake up.

You can always rationalize a marriage, though, seeing it as a means for finding out what sort of man your wife would have preferred. So, like a very dull dinner . . . with dessert at the beginning . . . marriage becomes a litany of love, hate, lies, jealousy, excruciating domestic boredom, and reciprocal destruction. When I asked one of my wives *why* she'd married me, she said she'd had a big fight with her family and she wanted to do something to disgrace them.

It's an impossible arrangement that sometimes works, this emotional garrison duty called marriage, a series of diminishing expectations that come about when a man steps into a snare of his own delusive making. Marriage is a price men pay to make a housekeeper *think* she's a householder. And marriages dissolve so often because a man has many more temptations than a woman—and the reason for that is, he knows where to find them.

I will now overwhelm you with my final, energetically malevolent definition: Marriage is the only sport, the only great adventure open and available to the craven and cringing . . . marriage is the last frontier for the docile explorer, and few men face it without remembering what happened to Livingston.

> *Beware the potential marriage*
> *partner who, like a child, expects*
> *to have every wish instantly*
> *gratified, no matter how unreasonable.*

Warming Up—
Indecision and Economic Considerations

Let us assume you are undergoing the sweaty dread of another lonely day and are ready to commit marriage. Love has crumpled your resistance like the happy clunk of a nightstick on the skull of a shambling wino. I urge you to proceed as carefully as a splay-footed cow on a trestle bridge. Indecision and economic considerations will soon find you mumbling perplexed incantations to yourself and becoming as sensitive as litmus paper to her shifting moods. Let me, your friendly nabe nit-picker and founder of the Most Ancient Order of Stonehenge Druids, suggest a few timely observations. If you pay attention now, later you won't feel as if you've been gutted by a meteorite.

A fool and his money are soon married, and even though it may be true that a woman doesn't exactly marry a man for his money, she may, on occasion, admit that it's nice to know there's always something about him she can like, one lonely redeeming trait.

First of all, there are only two kinds of wives . . . those who have rich husbands and those who act as if they have. At the same time there's nothing that can take the sting out of marriage like an upper-bracket romance, although any man who marries for money really earns it because his wife punishes him from that moment on for not marrying her for herself.

Some marriages fail because a man works only five days a week, but a woman spends money seven days a week. So how can we say talk is cheap, when the two words, "I do," cost a man at least half of everything he owns and earns?

Ever notice that some wives leave their husbands and take everything . . . others take everything but don't leave? This state of affairs can generate true resentment in a man . . . to such an extent that he won't even declare his wife a dependent on his income tax return.

Some girls do marry for love ... they love the way a man spends money on them. But, then, if men acted after marriage the way they do before marriage, there'd be a lot fewer divorces but many more bankruptcies. Often, however, when a man is generous, the *last* one to find out is his wife.

After all, why should a man get married when he can have the whole show just for the amusement tax? In a typical marriage, economic dependency parades as wifely devotion, and the whole depraved fantasy becomes instantly clear when he comes home with lipstick on his new jacket and his wife demands to know where he got the money for that new jacket.

I'd never mislead you, girls, so here's my advice: Never hesitate to marry a rich old guy—you know, the May and December syndrome. It's an even trade—May has all the freshness of springtime but December has Christmas.

As for you men: Marry a poor girl if you want to settle down, and a rich girl if you want to settle up. Remember that the man who originated the saying, "Two can live as cheaply as one," died of malnutrition. That's because to most girls, the ideal man is a guy who is *smart* enough to make money, and *dumb* enough to get married. Muggers demand either your money or your life ... wives demand both. Which reminds me, a diamond is the hardest substance known to man ... to get back.

It is written as Ballance's Law that the most disillusioned girls are those who married because they were tired of working. This makes a wife the world's most costly roomie, and by the time a husband discovers what a wife saw in him, it's all spent. That's because a woman picks a man just the way she shops ... the first item she's shown is something to keep in mind while she looks around for a better deal.

A woman needs at least one man on whom to test her sense of power, and he is always the wrong man for her to marry.

In most instances, two can live more cheaply than one wants to, and if you don't believe in buried treasure, just listen while some widows talk about their first husbands. In fact, there's a new perfume out now—hyper-secret formula, smells like money—it makes a man imagine he can support a wife. Of course, always pity the man who marries for love and then discovers his wife has no money.

But a man can spend so much money on a girl that he has to marry her . . . for his money. I know. Can a man list divorce expenses on his income tax as home improvement? Don't count on it, Pal.

Just remember that the bonds of matrimony are nonnegotiable, and that a wife is a woman who gets more pleasure from spending money than her husband gets from earning it.

Naturally, girls, you wouldn't marry a man for his money . . . but keep in mind that you want your husband to have a good disposition, and if he were poor he'd be all worried, irritable, sick, and nervous.

A recent carefully slanted survey proves that people who live the longest are rich old husbands. Remember Ballance's queasy quatrain:

> Wives who cook and swab the dishes
> Must be granted these three wishes—
> A grateful stud, a well-kissed cheek,
> And taken out three times a week.

As we embark on the seas of rapture for the islands of desire, here's an observation induced by the seasoned wariness of a man who's been there: God help the man who won't marry until he finds the perfect woman, and God help him even more if he finds her.

> *An astute gentleman can*
> *read a woman like a book . . .*
> *but only to himself.*

Commitment

How to Select a Spouse

And now, thrill-seekers, I shall administer Extreme Unction to your womanly anguish with the word on how to avoid being scorched with desire, mangled with unrequited passion, benumbed by loneliness, a victim of unfocused fantasies, crushed by your own coquettishness. As Champion Long-Distance Grudge Keeper, I assure you that if you insist on becoming a master in the art of romantic indolence and cannot overcome that inertia of the spirit which results in matrimony, you had best pay mighty close heed.

My active life has furnished me the following rules, which should be applied to the selection of your own personal life partner. Basically, for you saucy brazens in the throes of emotional saber rattling, it would be best to select a husband the same way you buy a dress. Do you want it simple and plain, like him, or hotshot funkadelic like his rival? This way you avoid anxiety and other random female ailments.

Rule 1: Scrutinize the material. Is it a new *synthetic* blend or a natural fiber? Is it aerodynamically flawless? Is it see-through (for those who have nothing to hide)? What are those suspicious stains?

Rule 2: Examine the design, look for unfinished hems, dangling threads, and frayed ends. Is it cut on the bias? Are its sleeves long to cover narco tracks?

Rule 3: Is it handmade or assembly-line produced? Was it made on a Monday morning, or a Friday afternoon? How sturdy is that balsa-wood crotch?

Rule 4: Make sure it has deep pockets which are easily accessible to long, tapered fingers; how come he likes black? Is he in mourning for his lost principles? Is this jumpsuit embroidered with lewd pornopatches?

A woman picks a man just the way she shops: The first item she's shown is something to keep in mind while she looks around for a better deal.

Rule 5: Is it strictly seasonal? Is it evergreen? Are those reconditioned gravy-ravaged buttons? Is it doubleknit dynamite, or understated elegance? Does it stretch?

Rule 6: Determine carefully how it fits. Is an eiderdown butterfly bow-tie really smog-resistant? Is it reversible? Are those counter-culture tatters?

Rule 7: Is it a passing fad? Will it go out of style quickly? Does it have a phony label? Does it project culture lag or future shock? Is it *vented* in the right places?

Rule 8: Will it stand up under repeated washings? Will it shrink; is it hard-working, long-playing material? Is it biodegradable? Is it big enough to accommodate his pebblegrain frisbee?

Rule 9: Make sure you have the right accessories and that you will be able to get long use out of them. Do not acquire anything that will clash with your current possessions (including your birthmark and wallpaper) or render them useless. Make certain none of your girl friends have the same model. Is the material *certified checked?*

A husband is like a garment: If a wife attempts too many alterations, she'll have nothing left but scraps.

Now, for you studs out there who are being neo-productive in the crucible of captivation, you vintage paramours who are weary of recrimination and reproach and of the malodorous vapors of romantic intrigue and chicanery who finally decide that your lives are one wild, negatively ruinous sequence of confusion and misdirected energy . . . may I remind you that we lead auto-motivated lives; so if your dollbaby has you hovering like a hummingbird before the delphinium, mark my words, you had better examine that potential wife the same way you buy an automobile. An ideal husband is one who treats his wife like a *new car.*

Rule 1: Listen to the engine . . . is it a new rotary job? Do those valves need regrinding? How is the compression?

Rule 2: Examine the chassis, look for weak points and bad connections. Load-leveler OK? How is its ATC rating? (Approach to Coroner).

Rule 3: Investigate the manufacturer's reliability. Has this model ever been *recalled* for adjustments? Perhaps to an overhead Camelot?

Rule 4: Check the ignition system; be sure the spark is active, but not likely to burn out. Can you bridge that spark plug gap efficiently? How does it behave on a lube rack?

Rule 5: How about those headlights . . . high beam or low beam? Do they give a dim? Are there any burnt-out fuses? Will those headlights dim unto others as you would have them dim unto you?

Rule 6: Examine that closed-state circuitry. Is it spring-operated and tension set? Is the solonoid perforated?

Rule 7: Observe fuel consumption. Is it only a high-octane performer, or will it run on regular? Have the tire treads been scrubbed out with a toothbrush?

Rule 8: Determine carefully how the model in question responds to your personal touch; has it been serviced in too many pit stops? Does it have an inflamed magneto?

Rule 9: If this is not a new model, find out for sure how it was treated in the past. Did it survive a demolition derby? Was it ever wrecked? Will it collapse under stress? Do obstacles make it ping annoyingly? Will its hidden flaws emerge just when you need it most? Do the loudspeakers emit a stereo stream of invective?

Rule 10: Compare carefully with competing models; take out for a series of demonstration drives. Does it tend to overheat under pressure? Is it self-lubricating? Can you guide it with one hand? How does it function at idling speed? Does it stall? Does it rev up quickly?

Rule 11: Are its shock absorbers efficient? Can it absorb shock without having to be sent back to the factory? Has it ever belonged to *ZAG*—"Zero Automobile Growth"?

Rule 12: Make sure the main bearing is the manufacturer's original and not a rebuilt job.

Rule 13: Finally, keep in mind that a modern automobile is like a fretful wife—it can irritate you to madness with a hundred unidentifiable complaints in its too highly developed insides.

Continue your emotional scenario, prattle endearments at her, lurch along beside her like a haggard mastiff, and let these convenient rules help reroute any further frenzies of self abasement and postpone those inevitable confrontations filled with tears and integrity.

> *Early in life you must choose*
> *between honest arrogance and*
> *hypocritical humility; you'll*
> *feel better if you're able to*
> *maintain invulnerable arrogance*
> *under intense pressure. When*
> *accused of being conceited, merely*
> *reply, "I am* not *conceited—*
> *it's just that I have*
> *MASSIVE SELF-RESPECT."*

June . . .

June is a state of mind that can create anxiety and other amatory aches, for a June wedding can ruin a man's summer vacation. It's the month when many a beautiful girl says she'll marry a big millionaire or nothing . . . and she gets half her wish; she marries a big nothing. June is the marriage month . . . when a girl's hardest task is to prove to a man that his intentions are serious. It is a month that usually begins in a whirling blur of joy and ends in subdued whimperings for clemency.

A time of amorous gamesmanship, June is the month when a girl goes from saying, "I do," to, "You'd better!" June is the favorite month for weddings for one main reason . . . after a long marriage, a couple can always look back to their wedding day and know that at least there was good weather.

Just remember, however, not all of those people carrying suitcases around town are tourists. Some of them are June brides going home to mother.

> *Life consists in what*
> *a person is thinking*
> *all day.*

Ballance's Recipe I: How to Preserve a Husband

Let us assume you are plagued by shredded nerves, tension, insomnia, anxiety, mental anguish, and rancorous hatred. You are, of course, married, and you're engulfed in a prolonged fit of remorse. You have weathered your surging fits of indecisiveness and decided to improve your tacky little life. For you charmers, the steps to happiness are as useless as a steam shovel without a lower lip, unless you observe the following hints on the half-shell. I enjoy food references because I have a great appetite; I take an elemental, purring pleasure in food, and I've always had a ravenous appetite for life itself; luckily, I have the digestion of a burro. Here's that recipe for your rapscallion:

First: Hopefully you did not choose too young and raw. This potential entreé must be neither too fibrous nor excessively flaccid.

Second: When once selected, give your entire thoughts to pacification and preparation for domestic use. Some women unfortunately insist on keeping husbands pickled, others keep them in hot water; this makes them sour, hard to get along with, and often bitter, as if they've been cooked on a senile stove.

Third: Even the poorest varieties can be tenderized by garnishing them with patience and well-sweetened with kisses from your succulent, plum-colored lips.

Then: Wrap them in the mantle of love, keep warm with a steady fire of domestic devotion, and serve with hot apple pie. Keep in mind, however, Ballance's Love-Couplet—

> An apple pie without some cheese
> Is like a kiss without a squeeze.

Thus prepared, he will keep for years! But remember that *faith* is essential—in credit, love, or hash. If you forget, I'll let the air out of your eyeballs.

Ballance's Recipe II: How to Preserve a Wife

Adhering to this recipe will keep you busier than a mongoose at a cobra rally; so pay attention now, observe intensely like a thunderstruck understudy, and you may set sail confidently on the Great Circle Tour of connubial captivation.

First: Be careful in your selection; thump judiciously to ascertain ripeness. This delicacy must be edible but without excessive roughage, lest your enzymes scream in anguish.

Second: When once selected, devote enough time so that care and attention are obvious. Some men insist on keeping their wives in the kitchen, while others try to keep them on a budget; this makes them irritable, testy, acrimonious, and often claustrophobic to the point of restless roving off the reservation.

Third: Even the most questionable varieties can be made delectable by marinating in love laced with understanding, well-tempered with tenderness and unadulterated passion.

Then: Wrap them in a modicum of cheer, keep warm with a steady fire of natural affection, and serve with unrestrained solicitude. If you follow this recipe, adding a pinch of fantasy, you will never again have to devote yourself to full-time woman troubles; henceforth, you will avoid the usual dreary sequence of remonstrance, violence, and, finally, icy withdrawal and sullen misery.

Thus prepared, she should be preserved indefinitely. But remember, there's a vast difference between making a Peach Cordial, and making a Peach Turnover.

> *A gentleman from the word Go is*
> *usually some guy who has just been*
> *asked to leave.*

Disillusion—
The Honeymoon Is Over When . . .

Well, curiosity seekers, if your blood sugar is running low and that encircling ring of savage mediocrity is closing in, you are probably on the verge of a highly personal apocalypse. This can make you meaner than a porcupine with ingrown quills. Keeping up that affable charade becomes rougher than a stucco bedpan. But there are ways to tell if you are connected with a Diesel-operated dullard, and most of the first clues come soon after your original quivering passion has left you on the brink of apoplexy.

Certain tormented traumas let you know the honeymoon is over. It is this state of affairs when the groom says he isn't worthy and the bride agrees. Or he stops helping her with the dishes and does them himself.

Maybe he stays out all night and she doesn't know it, or the dog brings his carpet slippers and his wife barks at him. His new bride suddenly goes from, "Yes, dear," to, "You'll do nothing of the kind," or the husband takes his wife off a pedestal and puts her on a budget. These are tip-offs to inherent deterioration and acute deprivation of delight.

This does not mean that the disintegration process is complete; it's just the first sign of romantic decay. She stops wearing falsies around the house, or he suddenly realizes that everything she says or cooks disagrees with him.

A real cruncher comes when his mother-in-law shows up for a weekend visit with six suitcases and the deed to her cemetery plot.

There always comes a time when a man wants to have words with his wife, but has no chance to use them, or she loses an argument and takes it to a higher court—her mother.

Have you ever been introduced with this phrase: "I want you to meet my present wife?" or, "This is my current husband, the Incumbent." If so, things look rocky, especially if he crawls into bed and reads about community property laws. Then there's the guy who refuses to quarrel with his wife but teases her by declining to come down off of the chandelier. This guy can instantly understand every word his wife is not saying.

How about the woman who says her husband has his *bad* faults and his *good* faults? She might say her husband is like something you see in a shop window . . . something she's always wanted, but when she got it home, she discovered it didn't go with the house.

A sure-fire way to tell if the honeymoon is over is when a man admits he's afraid to make up his mind until he's consulted his wife. There is also another method of deducing deterioration: When a wife discovers something to put in the dishwater that's guaranteed to keep her hands soft. It's called "husband's hands."

Girls, you know it's all over when your husband makes the same agonized sounds when parting with money that your Dad did. Better double check the situation when your ability to cook begins to seem important to him, or when your guy is

A real cruncher comes when his mother-in-law shows up for a weekend visit with six suitcases and the deed to her cemetery plot.

asked, "How's your wife?" and he answers, "Compared to what?"

Nervous is the man who notices that his lady has put her bikini top on backwards, and it fits. Indeed, the honeymoon is over when the bridegroom, who promised to tell his bride everything she ever wanted to know about sex, finds out she already knows.

This trauma can work two ways at once, when both parties come to a mutual misunderstanding. In this case, the honeymoon is over when the woman discovers that she didn't marry a big spender, and the man finds out that he did.

> *Sophistication is the art*
> *of knowing when to appear naive.*

You Really Know You're Married . . .
when these grisly episodes occur

Ever gone out driving with another couple and the wives sit together in the back seat? Did you stop buying regular Christmas cards and start sending pictures of you and the kids in front of the fireplace? Can your wife sign your signature on your paycheck better than you can? Is your idea of a great anniversary gift for yourselves a new hose for the vacuum cleaner? or a cover for the ironing board? If these seemingly trivial questions have produced a savage scowl on your perspiring brow and made you madder than a ballet dancer with gout, face it, chum, you must really know you're married.

Do you check into a hotel together and the clerk gives you twin beds without even asking? Do you look for your daily paper and find it spread out over the newly washed kitchen floor? Don't just throw up your hands in peevish dismay. I know how tough it is. A real groin-kicker, a knee in the machismo, right? I know, and now you know. You're emphatically married, and it's your own fault; your happiness has gone down the drain, and you're the guy who pulled the plug.

*Married couples are like
refrigerators—they slowly
gather an ice formation which, if
allowed to accumulate unchecked,
will reduce their effectiveness.
These people need occasional
defrosting.*

Observations

The Wife

Men, it's BB here with my official unfettered secret of happiness; learn to accept the impossible, to do without the indispensable, and to bear the totally intolerable; in other words, recognize your wife for what she is. If you've exhausted all your emotional reserves, if you've just come through and barely survived an obliterating experience of unbridled desire, only to find you've hooked up with a ruthless conniver, a conspiratorial cupcake, a relentless schemer, it is high time you looked at her with rechristened eyes. What is this thing called "wife" you might ask. I'm here to clarify the character of this wistful wench you're married to, that woman who wheedled you into committing yourself to emotional bondage. After all, she's more than just that shrill, piping voice in your life, she's the cornerstone of this large, exquisitely interesting, meaty, fraught-with-significance chapter.

You must first realize that to a woman, the perfect husband is one who thinks he has a perfect wife. That's because a contented wife is one who can't think of a better man she could have married. By the way, the perfect wife is one who remains faithful, but tries to be just as charming as if she were not.

No matter how deeply in love you are with your wife, *never* rule out the possibility that you will ultimately have a spat and splinter apart, and that you both will peel off into the arms of someone else; when you know in your heart that she wants out, take her gingerly in your arms, gaze into her treacherous, guilty eyes and intone, "Babydoll, let us do nothing to inhibit and everything to facilitate the inevitable." She will be so astonished at your gentlemanly attitude, she might even consider trying to make a go of it again. *DON'T LET THAT HAPPEN* or *ALL IS LOST!*

When the wife insists on wearing the pants, some other woman wears the mink coat, right? Likewise, if you give a wife enough rope, she's just bound to skip. For all practical purposes, though, you men never really know how much your wives suffer—unless, of course, you listen. The best way to cure a wife of nagging is to remind her that nagging is a sure sign of encroaching age. This could create dangerous flashbacks though, since a wife is only a sweetheart with the trial period expired.

Many times, when a woman likes a man's company, she's not content to be just a shareholder—she marries him and becomes chairman of the board; no longer can he drink and sing and strut in the cool of the evening. She forbids it. This uncomfortable state of affairs, this pretty kettle of squid, is caused by one giant difference: Women *always* worry about the future until they have husbands, whereas men *never* worry about the future until they have wives. In a moment of weakness, when a fella needs a friend, a lot of times he gets confused and acquires a wife instead. From that point forward, the future ceases to reek with charm and becomes redolent of regret.

Some men don't send their wives candy and flowers like they did before they were married; you know why? Because she doesn't live with her parents anymore. Most of the time it pays to be tactful with your wife, though: Say, "Honey, we may be a little incompatible in a few minor areas, but basically you're all wrong."

There are times when circumstances have a way of inverting themselves, like when a man marries a girl thirty years younger than himself. It isn't her youth he is seeking, but his own.

Another piercing message that just flashed across the panel of my mind is an amiable rejoinder a man can make to a whining adversary: "Sweetheart, if I had my life to live over, I wouldn't change a single thing—except you." And if you want to be the hit of any party, introduce your wife as your "roommate." If you feel guilty, just remember that no wife ever sprains the thumb she holds her husband under.

Let us now pity those poor guys who are leading unhappy lives because the girl they once loved ran off and got married . . . to them. Let us recognize that ideal wives are those who know intuitively when their husbands want to be forced to do something against their will. That's because most men control their wives about as much as a weather vane controls the weather. Still, I know one movie exhibitor who digs his wife so much, he's decided to hold her over for another year.

Don't ever worry though, men, anytime you want your wife to really listen to you, just start whispering to a strange girl at a party.

All this antagonistic skirmishing could be avoided if a man realized that a wife, like a radio, should be chosen by ear rather than by eye, because after marriage, a man usually stops looking at a woman but he can't stop listening to her.

And never forget—a woman will believe *anything,* if it's about her husband.

Here's a little remark you murmur to a pesky, irritating wife: "Listen, our marriage would be a lot more pleasant without you!" Or you can try to keep your wife punctual by saying: "While I wait for you, my dear, I spend the time thinking of your faults." Attitudes like this are generated by the fact that not all women devote their time and energy to trying to please men; some of those women are married.

Remember that a wife is always saying that she and her husband like the same things. But she forgets to mention that it took him fifteen years to learn. Many men think of their wives like they do their religion . . . neglected, but always there. And of course, farm girls make great wives because no matter what happens, they've seen worse.

Good manners play an important part in the husband-and-wife drama. You dudes must realize that the only time it's polite to talk with your mouth full is when you're praising your wife's cooking. Thus, a housewife needs strong nerves, an instinct for intramural combat, the hide of a rhinoceros, and the willingness to work like a dog for an occasional rain-washed bone. Face it, a housewife is a domestic drudge, sentenced to life at hard labor for stealing a heart. That's why a wife can be so moody; she has so many ups and downs, her man has to hop alertly through life on a Pogo stick. So you guys with a chronically nagging wife, here's what to say to her every morning: "Get up dear, you have a whole day of *complaining* ahead of you."

The man who has everything doesn't have a wife . . . if he did have a wife, he wouldn't *have* everything. That's because a wife is a frequent and unabashed sparring partner who will listen to reason only if she's thinking of something else. Where it takes a real man to admit he's wrong, it takes a wife to point it out and keep reminding him of it.

A modern wife is one who puts off today what her maid can do tomorrow. This is the kind of wife you should put on a pedestal . . . like when the ceiling needs painting. Of course, if TV doesn't get better at night, a lot of men may go back to listening to their wives, and maybe even watching them again.

Isn't it ironic that many a girl who hates housework can be persuaded to sweep down an aisle? In a burst of generosity, a clever wife sees through her husband, while a wise wife sees him through. This is the sign of a happy marriage: She likes her husband better than almost anyone else's.

This conjures up an image of the perfect wife in my mind: A girl who looks like Candice Bergen, has a figure like Raquel Welch, spends money like Jack Benny, eats like a parakeet, and works like an ox. Unfortunately, most wives are the sort that listen to reason, but not the same one too often; they stay close to him at parties so they can ignore him better, and if the poor devil starts talking to an attractive girl, she gives him one of those "married looks."

But if American men are *not* spoiling their wives, it's

about time they found out who is. Most wives tell their husbands everything . . . at least everything they're sure to find out anyway.

I recall a man who met his wife when he was a lifeguard at the beach. He figured that she wasn't really drowning, and was tricking him into meeting her. Why else would she go swimming in a white bridal gown? This same predatory woman braves chilly wintry blasts in a micro-mini, but requires 90 percent of her poor husband's blankets.

There are many ways to make a wife happy. Two of the most important are: A faithful husband, and someone to compare him with often—so, men, for her next birthday, give her a secret lover. Remember that it's not who you are that counts, but how your wife found out. Incidentally, if you're living with your wife's parents, the best birth-control device is a bed that squeaks.

A midwife is the second of three wives; a *good* marriage counselor can tell a man how to get along with a woman . . . without his wife getting wind of it.

The authentic test of a happily married (and wise) woman is whether she can say, "I love you" more often than she asks, "Do you love me?"

The real secret of marriage, though, is that a man's wife murders him every day, and then gets him to apologize for it. So let your wife know that you think about her occasionally . . . grind your teeth and growl, and make fists at her in your pockets.

Most men like their wives to be just clever enough to comprehend their cleverness, and just stupid enough to admire it.

Home cooking is where many a man thinks his wife is. Look at it this way: A wife can get resigned to a dull married existence after a few years . . . she plods stolidly through what remains of her life and gradually becomes similar to an old cow which placidly accepts kicks on its spavined flanks. These women are hard to impress, naturally, unless of course you talk in your sleep. Then she evolves into a suspicious, jealous wife who serves at least one good function: If it weren't for her, unattractive secretaries would never get jobs.

She evolves into a suspicious, jealous wife, who serves at least one good function; if it weren't for her, unattractive secretaries would never get jobs.

Fortunately, in America, a man is not allowed to have more than one wife . . . it's the way the law protects those who are incapable of protecting themselves.

Nothing is so gratifying to a wife as seeing a double chin on her husband's old girl friend. That's because succeeding as a housewife is about as easy as sewing a button on a poached egg. Which reminds me that a tremulously alert wife is one who always serves her husband breakfast in bed, because she'd rather do that than face him across the breakfast table. The same women probably asks herself if a middle-aged housewife can find happiness with a twenty-year-old . . . bottle of Scotch.

A man's *mother* is his unavoidable misfortune, but his wife is his own fault.

It's one of the really big problems of today, learning to live with other people; like wives, for instance. One of the reasons relates to when a woman first gets married; she is usually nervous and hysterical. After a few years, she only panics. So a man who says he would rather make love to his wife than eat may not think that she's such a beauty . . . she may be just a rotten cook.

That makes me think of an ex-friend who calls his wife a child bride, and I didn't know why until they invited me over for dinner. Have you ever tried being polite while eating low-cal mud pies? Makes you think that every man needs a wife because there are so many things in life that cannot be blamed on the government. So what if you rule the roost and she rules the rooster? If you are forced into home remedies, a good wife is best.

*A triangle is something
that occurs in social
circles when people are
not on the square.*

The Husband

Now all you girls out there, I want you to know that if your spirit is frustrated, full of atrophied amour and ossified estrogen because you can't understand why your husband has turned into a mottled, senile old crock of emulsified lard, this psychological dissection of the deadbeat will help you cope.

In other words, if you feel you're being tilted over the edge of a romantic precipice, if you're undergoing a major emotional transition or life crisis and need to redirect and refocus your heart in your search for deep-down visceral relief, allow the linkage of your head to be tightened by me, your amatory ombudsman.

About husbands: A husband is a sweetheart with the nerve removed. For a perfect husband, marry a burglar; he's trained himself to pick up things, and be quiet around the house. Of course when a married man dreams he's a bachelor it's a sure sign he's going to be disappointed when he wakes up, unless he's already done time and thrives on domestic penal servitude.

Honestly girls, there's only one way for you to acquire an ideal husband: Get him when he's four years old and spank him every day for pouting. As Kung Fu-tsu once said: "When heavy dude get married, he become subdued."

I know a man who's so henpecked his wife writes his diary a month in advance. That's due to the fact that women who constantly read their husbands like a book soon learn that some of the pages are stuck together. This could possibly relate to what a married man considers one of the biggest mysteries: What does a bachelor do with his money?

Pay attention girls, and don't waver. Give me your widest span of attention: The way to hold a husband is to keep him a little jealous; the way to lose him is to keep him a little more jealous. A wise woman makes her husband think he's head of the house, when actually he's only chairman of the entertainment committee. So a husband is a guy who lost his liberty in the pursuit of his happiness.

Most of you girls don't talk to your husbands except when they are reading, and you dominate them too much—if it weren't for the step-on garbage can, your husbands would never have a chance to put their foot down. But I assure you that I have a warm spot in my rectifier for every woman who is corralled by a guy who, before marriage, was seething with charm . . . and within hours after the ceremony became a clod with a chintzy heart. Of course you don't want some shallow simpleton who's grinning and scratching all the time either— some puny pipsqueak so relentlessly jovial he could giggle his way through a heart transplant.

Actually, some women are very happily married. The only things that annoy them are their husbands. The secret of some marriages is that neither one of them can stand him. This occurs when the man's self-image is a rimless zero; they both realize he's a human cipher.

A buddy of mine has to think carefully, *twice,* before he leaves his wife alone at night . . . first, he has to think up a reason for going out, and then he has to think up a reason why she can't go with him.

It's a cruel truism that when a man changes his mind as much as a woman, chances are he's married to her.

Some women give men the best years of their lives, and then they get married, and their husbands get what's left.

Mental leftovers are just as bad, though . . . just like the husband who gives his wife flowers; they are nothing more than the blooms of a guilty conscience.

But a man who gives in when he's wrong is wise . . . a man who gives in when he's right is married. Also, a man is never master of his own house until he can safely slam the front door at two in the morning. Then, if his wife ever asks, "Whatever became of the man I married?" he tells her, "The Indians killed him at Little Big Horn." But even as a last resort, a man should never strike his wife, except in self-defense, or until they have been properly introduced.

Attention, newly-married men: Be warned! You will soon learn that the most difficult task you face is to convince a woman that even a bargain costs money. So even if married men are not the *best* informed people, they are certainly the most informed, especially by me. For example, a husband can be sure his wife really loves him if she suggests that he use more room in the closet. And you know the real reason men marry beauti-ful-but-dumb girls: When she starts telling him his faults, he won't get an inferiority complex.

Utilizing some statistical irrelevancies at my disposal, I have found that it is a numerical fact that out of every ten married men living in the United States today, four of them are dead, and the others wish they were. As I undergo an acute attack of satyriasis, let me remind you that all married men should forget their mistakes . . . there's no use two people remembering them. Every husband should know that he will never live up to his wife's expectations, and the only time a husband can keep his wife guessing is when he's dancing with her.

The trouble with marriage is that while every woman is at heart a mother, every man is at heart a bachelor. You can tell immediately who is in charge by checking out the bedroom. If it's pink, it isn't him. And any husband who asks his wife for advice just hasn't been listening. Not surprisingly, this is directly related to the fact a lot of restless, roaming men think of their home only as a soup kitchen with a built-in kissing booth.

Personally I'm not hunting for the right girl anymore; I'm just doing the best I can with all the *wrong* ones, the more *predatory* the better. In a way, the happiness of a married man depends on the women he has *not* married. My agent, Sasha Deal, claims that he's the absolute boss in his house, and he says it's going to stay that way. He tells that to his wife while he's ironing her blouse.

But a genuinely happily married man is a guy whose personality remains unchanged whether his wife is with him or not. The opposite to this is a man who puts his foot down only because his wife has finished vacuuming under it. This type is called a mouse: Something a woman is afraid of until she marries one.

A guy with guts of pure titanium is one whose facial expression remains exactly the same when his wife tells him he's been talking in his sleep. So many women are married to misdirected, totally disorganized guys . . . energetic weaklings full of ambitious confusion, aggressive mediocrity . . . all bug and no lightning.

It's like the guy who told his wife that marriage and a career don't mix . . . so he's never worked. But what is a regular-type husband? He's a guy ranging in age from 15 to 105. He's

He's the absolute boss in his house, and he says it's going to stay that way. He tells that to his wife while he's ironing her blouse.

referred to as the Head of the House. He's a man who's learned to argue on a comparative basis, promise on a sliding scale, and reluctantly concede.

A man rarely knows what real happiness is until he gets married . . . and then it's too late. But where some old-fashioned mothers can remember their husband's first kiss, their swinging daughters can't even remember their first husbands.

The only time a lot of guys are ever even seen with their wives is after they've been indicted.

On the other hand, some men get so mixed up, disoriented, and confused after marriage that they couldn't even organize a two-car funeral. Why, if most women had it to do over, they'd marry men they didn't have to do over; for, indeed, it is written that many a big wheel at the office is a mere hubcap at home.

It isn't uncommon for some women to kiss their husbands only to see if they've been drinking; and the way a lot of men embrace their wives (gingerly) it looks as if they're afraid they might have to marry them again. And now meet the prudent husband: His wife hasn't spoken to him for a week and he's in no mood to interrupt her.

Any man can make a mistake, even though the man who gets married a third time isn't entitled to any sympathy whatsoever. When a man marries a third time, it's a triumph of hope over experience.

Ever notice how a man goes through a certain character alteration when he gets married? Before the ceremony, most guys pretend they have a remarkable gift of gall and bold brashness— full of masculine audacity—but after the wedding, he slips gradually into the role of little boy, needing protection from the bullies of real life and murderous competition. Like the guy who doesn't worry about bad breath, because since he got married he hasn't had a chance to open his mouth.

Well, girls, if your husband never actually takes a bath, four times a year have him sandblasted. As for you men, if you're *not* in love with another woman, you might as well be nice to your wife.

From the BBC—Bill Ballance Catechism: A lot of women love sports, until they marry one.

> *A housewife's life seems easy on the*
> *surface, but it is riddled with the*
> *nervous and emotional strain of*
> *having to be subservient to the petty*
> *needs of others; being a housewife*
> *is a grim daily drama of desire to*
> *live divided against itself.*

Dissolution

One of the neat and superficial things about being married is the way you two develop special ways of communicating, pet prejudices, secret glances of mutual significance; the way you share portions of your passionate past and private joys and dislikes. This is also one of the areas where things get exciting when it's fall-apart time. You girls start doubting the value of your existence, feeling that the man in your life has been raffling off your head and exacting dependent tribute from your susceptible heart. Put it this way: Your dream husband has turned out to be a dolt, a cad, and a bounder; you have forgotten Ballance's Law from his Dissolution Syllabus—the only way a woman can ever *reform* a man is by *boring* him so completely that he loses all possible interest in life.

As for you husbands, you might suddenly discover that you are legally and socially shackled to Miss Water Retention, a rouged-beyond-recognition, bloated facsimile of something that slipped your mind a few years ago. Start tallying up all that unvectored energy and targetless direction and you become aware of a badly shriveled love life, mired in the terrifying boredom and plastic security of married nonlife. If this is the case, it's Disintegration City, so get on the gloves and start reviewing every marvelous moment in clashing, strident unison.

Remorse in a deteriorating marriage is a sign that it wasn't quite as pleasant as you expected it to be. But listen, Sport, you *never* hear of a man marrying a woman to reform her. Usually, intrusive relatives (when I was married, I called them my Meddle-in-Laws) scuttle a marriage, for it is written as a Ballance Codicil that *any man who is a hero to his in-laws may face the rest of the world fearlessly.* And no man is a failure until his wife thinks so. Conversely, no man is a success until his in-laws grudgingly admit it.

Always be grateful to your vigilant neighbors. Just think, a marriage counselor gets $25 an hour to listen to a couple yelling and screaming and fighting. Neighbors do it for nothing.

By the way, a man who marries a second time didn't deserve to lose his first wife . . . that doesn't mean much when you first read it, but after you think about it awhile, it becomes totally fatuous and will give you emotional ascendancy over your peers. But confusion sometimes comes to middle age, when couples reach the Playboy stage of their marriage: He's folding up and she's folding out. That's because when you've been married a long time it's sort of like an old smudgepot . . . there may not be much flame in the orchard, but it's enough to keep the frost off the plums.

Sometimes, at a wedding, when she says, "I do," and he says, "I do," it's the last time they agree on anything. It would be great if husbands and wives could pull together through life, like teams of horses going up a steep hill . . . they probably could, too, if they had only one tongue between them.

In marriage you become trapped by emotional inertia. Sometimes a woman hopes that having a child will save her marriage . . . until her husband runs off with the baby-sitter. It's become a familiar complaint: "We became such average people, love became an everyday thing; life was so much fun when we were living together, but as soon as we put on those rings, everything changed."

You can usually rate your marriage like they do for movies:

G for grim, PG for pretty ghastly, R for regretted, and X for extravagant. Or you can have a brief marriage, like a typical Hollywood couple that was joined asunder; they saved a piece of their wedding cake for the divorce lawyer.

But you know right from the start that you are in trouble when, at the marriage ceremony, your mother-in-law says, "*We* do." It also pays to remember that there is no Geneva Convention covering home arguments. Along these lines, there is one thing that a marriage can teach you: To think things far enough ahead not to say them.

The true mark of a happy marriage, though, is a one-woman man and a one-man woman, and each weekend the four of you get together and have a ball.

Just remember, you insatiable hedonists, that half of our marriages are dying in bed, possibly because after seven years, there seems to be a paucity of communication . . . you've told each other everything you know, your entire life stories, and you just lie there, your eyes going blank like owls in the daytime.

I've got something to say about those computer marriages, too. The problem with a computer marriage is that the bride and groom have to promise not to fold, staple, mutilate, or punch each other. But without those stimulating ingredients, no marriage can survive.

Listen, curiosity seekers, marriage does something to a love affair anyway; it takes something intriguing out of it; there's a certain thrill about unmarried love, a sort of advance-and-retreat challenge, when two people know they can leave each other; and that feeling never exists inside the circle of a wedding ring. Face it, when a marriage is on the rocks emotionally, esthetically, and sexually, it's foolish not to end it legally. Marry in haste . . . repent insolvent.

We all know that the most critical period in matrimony is breakfast time, but if we men knew how women pass the time when they're *alone,* we'd never get married in the first place. One friend of mine found his wife taking singing lessons, for example, and now he has to stand out in the yard every time she starts to practice because he doesn't want the neighbors to think he's beating his cocker spaniel.

There's nothing like an innocent, early marriage, though. Usually, it's enough to make hair grow on your eyeballs when you look back on it with the usual terror. When two teenagers get married, you know, the *only* one who lives happily ever after is the marriage counselor.

There are really only three kinds of marriage: Trial marriage, companionate marriage, and fight-to-the-finish.

He who hesitates has been married before. I know a guy who has lived through the perfect arrangement: One night a week, he's allowed to go out with the boys, while the other six nights, she goes out with them. This is the woman who wears her wedding ring on the wrong finger, because she married the wrong man.

Look at it this way: Sex started the bonfire, your children's dependence kept it burning, and your paycheck furnished the draft that kept the embers glowing long after the flame died out. In this situation the lady of the cave is likely to lodge a familiar complaint: When they first got married, he looked like Cary Grant: Now, after years of honest service, she says he looks like General Grant. She used to look like a Greek goddess, now she looks like a Greek waitress.

The main reason for unhappy marriages is that men cannot fool their wives the way they could fool their mothers. But parents aren't always so slow, like a friend of mine knew he was in trouble the minute he was married because his wife's mother and father sent him a thank-you note. In his case, "Here Comes the Bride" was the prelude to a lifetime of dedicated litigation.

Some complexities defy analysis, like the Hollywood couple who decided to get married but couldn't agree on a wedding list because they'd already married all of their friends.

I know one actress who hated her husband so fiercely that when he suddenly died she insisted on being present at his autopsy; she stood there smiling and softly strumming her guitar as his skull was peeled back and his insides were extracted and plopped on the drain table.

A typical lovers' quarrel takes place when *she* wants a big wedding and *he* wants to break the engagement. A good reason for this might be that she's been married so often the only thrill she could get out of Niagara Falls would be to go over them in a barrel.

In the last analysis, remember that the thing a man gets most out of marriage is himself. Just think of it, you dudes out there poring over these prescient pages, a few words mumbled over your head and you're married . . . a few words mumbled in your sleep and you're divorced. What the hell, a marriage always disintegrates when it is only a partnership in sex, play, and conspicuous expense. So if you're able to hang on to your sanity after extricating yourself from a disastrous marriage, give yourself some assurance. How? By reminding yourself that emerging from a rough divorce is like climbing gingerly off a tiger's back and being grateful that you lived to tell about it.

Marriage comes in on a white horse and goes out on a nag. It is a holy deadlock, the bitter taken with the sweet. The wedding ring is a matrimonial tourniquet, designed to stop circulation. But sometimes a marriage has a happy ending: Everyone is glad that it's over.

The secret of success
is the willingness
to make enemies.

Rules for Remarriage

You might know the rules of the road, Sport, but the rules for remarriage are different from the gruntheaded guidelines you smitten lovebirds use the first time. Considering that every third American couple unties the knot (every other couple, if you happen to make your bed in California), this section falls under the heading of public service.

Rules For Men:

1. Don't marry anyone who isn't *getting* in child support at least what you're *paying out.* That would be poor money management.

2. Make sure the home you'll be moving into is just as comfortable as where you used to live, but not next door.

3. If your last wife was a porker with charging rhino haunches, with great quivering gelatinous waffle-thighs, take your candidate for next wife to restaurants renowned for their pastry. Watch carefully her dessert selection and notice if she finishes yours in a burst of growling gluttony.

4. If your last mother-in-law lived down the block and was widely known as Godzilla, choose a new wife whose family, (a) lives out of town, or (b) is happily deceased and enriching the soil.

5. If your former wife went to the zoo and saw only the minks, look for a girl who pickets to protest the slaughter of furry animals for coats; that way, your wallet will never become an endangered species.

6. And if your ex demonstrated her cooking skill by serving baked gopher-loaf twice a week, look for gourmet girls who won't accept a date on the night Julia Child's on television. Also, casually clutch your new girl by the seat of her skivvies and say you admire her teflon bottom. That's the only way to check her knowledge of skillets.

Rules For Women:

1. Only consider a man whose monthly salary *exceeds* what you will *lose* in alimony. Also, find out what he pays in alimony. If these figures don't come out right and you are still interested in him, discreetly scout around for men who will take out his ex-wife and perhaps commit matrimony with her, and thus get her off your man's back.

2. Observe life-style. If your former husband dragged you to every social event within an eighty-mile radius because he sold insurance and it was "good for business," do not hang out with stockbrokers and other hustlers with similar fiscal dependencies. Also, is he cleaner than that first wretch, who had to have his socks chiseled off twice a year?

3. Know your prospects before you scramble aboard. For example, if you were always annoyed by your ex-husband's girl friends, old or current, look carefully at your new lover; if he is festooned with blazing kissing hickies *not* placed by you, beware.

4. Don't repeat the same old patterns. If your ex-husband always ended quarrels by blackening both of your eyes, check around to learn if your friend's former wife often wore shades after dark, and got royalties from Erase.

5. And it's vital for you to be vigilant; watch his reaction when you two are having dinner at a fancy restaurant and you sit there tossing onion rings over the candlestick. If he bellows at you to stop, that means he's pompous and stuffy and you certainly don't want that again.

> *Life is the art of* drawing *without*
> *having to use an* eraser.

Miscellaneous Tips

These are just random ruminations, points to ponder, especially for you girls with perky heads, for I know that among those bobbypins, that ballpoint hairdo, the perfume (there's a new perfume for prudish spinsters: "That's-all-you-men-think-about #5"), and problems, there's an incisive mind churning with great expectations. Remember that a marriage license is a legal paper (a two-dollar operation to have your backbone removed) which lets you keep the game in captivity after the hunting season. For those of you experiencing the pangs of passionate intensity, if you marry in haste, you will lose your leisure. That's because a lot of men who propose on bended knee still haven't gotten back on their feet.

Marriages may be made in heaven, ladies, but man is responsible for the maintenance work. Many a happy marriage is due to the fact that they are both in love with the same woman. Love can survive anything, sweetheart, but marriage. The reason for this searing truth is that to a woman at 18, marriage is an adventure, at 22 a career, at 30 a goal, and at 40 a haven.

Most women marry the first time for love, the second time for companionship, the third time for support, and the rest of the time from habit.

Remember, there is nothing on earth people are more suspicious of than a happily married couple. But things aren't what they used to be anymore, thank God. Kids, for example, don't wait . . . the bride is given away by her father, not to mention her waistline. But when it comes to marriage proposals, a girl listens a lot faster than a man talks. So that way brides are not really happy . . . just triumphant.

Whatever you do, my dear, don't get married impulsively . . . hold back and think about it. You'll discover that when we have second thoughts about something, our first thoughts don't seem like thoughts at all, only feelings. As for a man, I think he should always be in love, and that is the reason he should never

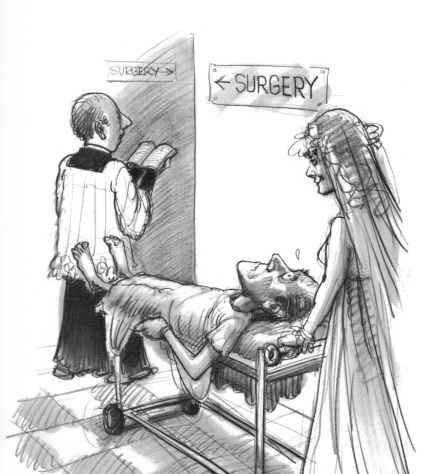

Remember that a marriage license is a legal paper, a two-dollar operation to have your backbone removed.

marry. If he does slip into the noose, he'll find out that the days before marriage are like a hip and jovial preface to a long, dull book.

Searching for a mate is like bobbing for apples . . . you never know when you'll come up with a worm.

Whatever you do, though, don't overanalyze your marriage . . . don't keep asking yourself if you're really happy . . . it's like yanking up a fragile indoor plant every twenty minutes to see how its roots are growing. I'll admit that most marriages are happy, but it's the living together afterward that causes all the trouble.

Remember, men, it is always dangerous to marry a woman who looks good in a black dress; which reminds me, have you ever noticed how some widows have such a majestic and noble bearing and overwhelming bravery, it makes their husbands seem especially dead?

But it takes two good liars to make a happy marriage. A man, for example, tolerates buying a house for the sake of the woman, while the woman tolerates the man for the sake of the house; but I want to emphasize this immutable fact—a couple's move from apartment to house means a subtle switch from male to female domination in their relationship. The woman has conned him into the commitment of "settling down." But then we all know that for a bride, a wedding means showers; for a groom, it means curtains.

So you guys pay strict attention, and never propose to a girl in a smoky, dimly-lit nightclub . . . many a guy selects a wife in subdued lighting that he wouldn't buy a cheap suit in. Don't think the girl will be nervous, though, because to some women, getting nervous at the prospect of marriage would be like a steeplejack getting scared while climbing a flight of steps.

Politics doesn't make strange bedfellows, marriage does. Ironic, isn't it, that the same people who say tobacco and alcohol are bad for you, claim that marriage is good for you.

Anyway, a marriage license no more makes a good spouse than a driver's license makes a good driver, and nothing gives a man that *closed-in* feeling like being caught in the middle of a wedding ring.

Don't overanalyze your marriage; it's like yanking up a fragile indoor plant every twenty minutes to see how its roots are growing.

The one sure way you girls can stop a man from making love to you all the time is to marry him. It might strike you as peculiar that I think everyone should be married: But not to each other. Whatever you do, though, don't get married too young, or you'll regret it to your dying day, if you should live so long. And never blurt out a marriage proposal . . . you'd be a victim of your own emotional impetuosity; girls often accept a guy's sudden marriage proposal on the wings of her first orgasm after a little ecstatic friction on the back seat.

As to you married women who complain about other women making out with your husbands . . . don't worry: You've got the bonfire, they're just getting a few sparks.

Marriage is that mighty thin line between love and hate, and most have been, or will be, tightrope walkers.

Many a homespun girl begins to unravel when she gets married.

Many a man who falls in love with a bosom makes the mistake of marrying the entire girl.

It pays to remember that marriage is only when every other line fails, and that success in marriage is much more than *finding* the right person . . . it is also *being* the right person.

As I said early on in this popular book, now in its *fifth* printing (the first four were blurred)—I was married twice to two different attractive women, both of whom were twenty when I married them. I was a rotten husband, but now I'd be a great one because I finally know myself. But why should I get married? I am the only guy I know who is living exactly the way he wants to and is making a living doing what he enjoys most—broadcasting five hours a day in the most competitive market on this troubled planet. I'm in radiant good health, which I regard as the most important thing in life, and am having a ball; I urge you to let yourself have a nifty time of it, too. Remember Ballance's Mortality Maxim: *Time, Divided by Life, Equals Death.* It's a lethal equation for all of us, with the exact time as the unknown. I know what I just said is fairly profound because my typewriter just reared back and gave me an inky soul-kiss. All of us, within ourselves, carry the seed of our own destruction; our bodies are clocks, slowly running down; every man's life ends the same way. It is only the details of how he lived and how he died that distinguishes one human from another. Every human being is put on Earth condemned to die—exact time, place, and method of execution unknown. We are racing toward the stars while creeping to the grave. I've already written my will. It starts off: "Being of sound mind, I spent it all. . . ."

The secret of success
is the willingness to
make enemies.

Chapter Four
Personality
and How to Detect It or
Appearance, Attitudes,
and Etiquette

If you're being duped, flimflammed, and swindled in the Con Game of Life, if you're being emotionally gypped, if you're being horn-swoggled and rooked through cunning deception, funky fraudulence, dazzling deceit and duplicity, let there develop method in your mendacity through careful and intense focus on this chapter which explores the process of selection.

If, for example, there were just one sunset every twenty years, how would people react? If there were just ten seashells in all the world, what would they be worth? If people could make love just once a year, how much more carefully would we select our mates? Each person is unique, and each person has his/her own special value. Only two things surprise me any-more: The way lightning strikes, and the people who marry each other; so that's why I say live together—don't get married; it's more daring and adventuresome. It's economically, emotion-ally, and sexually advantageous. Marriage is unnecessary, and it's hypocritical because of easy and rampant divorce or dissolu-tion. Life is now, today, and nothing is permanent, especially fragile human relationships. I have a fierce respect for the individual, for his right to happiness on the job as well as in personal relationships; I feel you should have a choice—when you live together, you do so because you *want* to, not because there's a legal document saying you *must.* Because of my intense love of freedom, and because of the infinite number of options in life, I want to leave as many options open as possible. I have never liked the state's role in human lives; the formality of a wedding ceremony is falling in line behind state-ordered dogma. Hell, I don't want to sign up for a year of *dance* lessons, let alone a marriage contract.

Personality is that magnetic outward expression that makes a person appear to be listening to what you say. What we want to prevent are football romances: Where each one is waiting for the other to kick off. Or those garden romances, where you wind up being a dead beet for an old tomato.

It is necessary, therefore, to reappraise yourself each month in reference to your efficiency, strategy, capability, and vulnerability. It is likewise important to ignore what people think. What people call you behind your back is not your business, but theirs. Just don't let anybody talk you into being a bum; always remember that your brains and your character are your true inventory. And learn as much as you can; remember Ballance's Law of Mental Acquisition: You are never paid for what you don't know.

Both brains and character can surface in strange ways at odd times, though, which reminds me of the time I once offered to buy a very sweet and innocent girl a drink, but she refused because she said she "never touched spirits." So I offered her a smoke, but she refused that too, because she never smoked. As a last resort, I offered her a chew of tobacco, but even then, she'd only take a little bite.

The key to character is attitude and style. I remember when a buddy and I used to own a 1931 Model A roadster, for example, and we'd take turns with our girls in the rumble seat. Making love in a rumble seat was always a lot of fun, especially in the summertime, when the lid was up. I am now chairman of the national committee to bring back rumble seats, especially if they're attached to a car.

My message is simple and basic. Whatever remarks release people and bring them together is good; whatever remarks confine or separate people is bad. Even so, rejection is hard to take. Some men and women just have a peculiar emotional effect on each other. Separately, they are able to keep themselves under control, but when they're together, they infect one another with whatever sort of tension each of them might be feeling at that particular moment, and it builds up into hysterical combat, often called marriage.

If a guy just happens to be dating a captivator though, and he needs a few sinister clues regarding the process of being wound down or phased out, here are some helpful hints: It's all over when you go out to a cocktail lounge and she insists on sitting at the bar instead of a table. It is also all over when you wave to a pal across the room, and she urges you to invite him over for a drink. If you try dancing cheek-to-cheek and she whines and grumbles that you're mussing her hairdo, it's curtains. A real tipoff, though, is at the end of the evening, when you ask her when you can see her again and she stands there yawning and scratching and says, "I can't tell you right now, so call me sometime next week, maybe, if you really want to."

I was once involved with a girl who sniveled, "That's how people get mono," every time I asked her for a kiss. Or when I'd suggest a little heavy cushion-pushin', she'd snarl, "Nah, that's kid stuff." When I wanted to hold hands, she'd say, "Holding hands make them sweat, and I hate that." When I wanted to turn off the lights, she'd say, "Whatsa matter, you tired of lookin' at my face?" When I wanted her to go out alone with me, just the two of us, she'd say, "But I like to mingle with crowds, and you don't look like no crowd to me." And every time I'd want to play davenport rugby or do a little indoor body surfing, she'd say, "Get yourself a reputation first." So now you know why our elopement was delayed indefinitely. I finally realized I was barking up the wrong leg.

Just remember, however, that the opposite can also hold true. If a devastating dollbaby says that you are kind, generous, considerate, and lovable, don't instantly break off the affair just because she forgot to say handsome and talented. That's what I did one time when I was giving my ego a happy run in the yard. If you are having problems, remember that the best way to save time when you're pursuing a girl, besides the usual exchanges of notes, hair, mottoes, and tumescent trinkets, plus protestations of undying love, is an occasional vague hint of a binding ceremony at the altar. Actually, I'm single after eleven years of random roving due only to my quick thinking, a few large closets, and an occasional fire escape. Of course, the main hazard in being a free-roving bachelor is waking up in the morning and wondering where you parked your car.

But why should I get married again? I'm getting all the sailing privileges without paying a docking fee. Once in awhile, I get disgusted at my pad over at Craven Manor, a terminal moraine of accumulated bachelor debris; the place is furnished in Early Scruffy; my kitchen has more dirty dishes than a hippie beauty contest, but I thrive on it, sitting there in the early morning sun, scratching myself shamelessly like an aging iguana. Squalor reigns unchallenged and I bask in comatose self-approval, surrounded by books and dusty mementos of earlier triumphs. Sure, I admit that my bachelor sty is a mess, but never forget that *order* breeds *habit,* whereas *chaos* breeds *life.*

You're not laughing much so far, but you are giving this book loving looks. So I'll level with you—I don't lead as wild a private life as you think. Frankly, my idea of an exciting Saturday night is to curl up with a good book and a glass of warm milk. The thrills and excitement come from trying to turn the pages without spilling the milk.

Appearances: For Girls Casing Guys

You think you can judge a book by its author? Well, if some guys are books, their indexes are scrambled, their appendixes are in the wrong place, and their bindings are loose. Does he listen with feigned, befuddled interest while he's standing there with his lank, oily hair down to his stoop-shoulder blades, wearing a grubby jumpsuit and no socks? Does he seem irretrievably third-rate? Is his grizzled mother an aging coquette full of shopworn dreams? Or is she a rampaging female jingoist sweathog? Does he project an almost combustible uncertainty, his head a shambles, seething with self-doubt and intimations of lifelong defeat? Is he from a family that's inbred to the point of imbecility? If his eyes are aglaze with the rudimentary intelligence of a cretinous tree sloth, if he's terrified of life and is ready at any moment to curl up into a quivering fearball and roll home to old Mom, beware. Look into the matter carefully. Is your man a victim of virulent *momism,* has his masculinity been undermined by a supermom from doublemotherland? If so, my darling, hop astride your swaybacked 10-speed and peddle hastily over the horizon. And while you're careening off into the mists, ask yourself, "Is he really the best I can do?"

Does he wear a magic crotcheted beanie under which he keeps his pet frog? Did a nearsighted Venus-flytrap rip the zipper off his pants? Does he croon softly to a small plaster statuette of a rock star, hoping thereby to generate a therapeutic burst of cosmic inspiration? Is he always groping for your candied yams, even in public? Is his complexion a sort of mottled pastel with streaks of ectoplasm that look suspiciously like snail trails? Does his skin break out constantly and look like a fruitcake that exploded in the oven?

There are other clues, too, sweetheart, like the kind of car he tools around in. Does he drive a runty foreign job called a

Flagel-8, which runs on fermented witch-hazel and acolyte sparkplugs? Does he live in a psychedelicized, multicolored VW van, steaming with rancid camaraderie? You can tell if he's a secret mamma's boy if he wears a thimble on his stick shift. Do little things go wrong with his car, like his horn doesn't blow, but the tires do, or his convertible top doesn't collapse, but the steering wheel does?

Some guys will do anything to get attention and keep up appearances. One dude I knew wore Supphose so tight, he had to take novocaine to get them on. Other guys look like fashion consultants for Goodwill. Still other men don't seem to be able to get themselves fitted correctly in anything. In his oversized turtleneck, he looks like a sparrow sitting in a wigwam; the same oaf invariably wears a sagging shirt, far too large so that it hangs around his pencil neck like a horse collar on a pump handle.

You can always tell the show-off, though, if he crams his body shirt all the way into his hypertight Gatsbys, and it's confined there by an irridescent gold lamé sash that brilliantly encircles his expanding waist, his machismo squirming like a snared rabbit. He loves to stride around, whacking his jodphurs with an obsidian riding crop and bragging about how he'll make millions out of his astute investment in Etruscan municipal bonds.

So shove this suggestion in your dainty reticule, sweetheart — probe his character carefully if you plan to get serious. Remember Ballance's Piercing Precepts, one of them being that the weakest spot in every man is where he thinks himself the wisest. But with most men, the greatest undeveloped territory in the world is between his ears. And never tie up with some bland, pusillanimous cipher; hunt for a man who is abundantly gifted and fiercely respected. Watch out for the phony posturing playboy, that pillar of jello, and be wary of eccentrics and cranks. To spell it out more concisely, an *eccentric* is a man who is a law unto himself; a *crank* is one who, having determined what the law is, insists on laying it down to others.

Be careful of the man who wears a rented watch or the clod who is so uncoordinated that when he yawns he has to try several times to cover his mouth once. Quirky weirdos can easily be spotted at the beach, and should be avoided. If you see somebody in the shallow end of the ocean wearing pale pistachio Teflon trunks that flare out at the knobby knees which look like Tinker Toy connections, if his seagoing costume includes sturdy, waterproof shinguards hooked to kapok clogs, you know what I'm talking about.

It usually pays to notice how a man carries himself, how he walks and moves and smells. If he has a peculiar gait sometimes you can attribute it to jockey shorts fastened to his boot buckles; and he might be wearing a pungent, highly effective new shaving lotion that grabs your attention and is driving you crazy with desire because it smells like a winning horse.

By all means don't get involved with one of those guys who is so scrawny that his muscles look like mosquito bites on a string of spaghetti. A guy like that will never be able to hold you tight enough or squeeze you properly. A certain inventiveness is always appreciated, though; you must admire the man who wears custom-crafted mentholated socks when he catches a cold. But resourcefulness can be overdone, like an oaf who feels compelled to prove his cleverness and adaptability by digging his hairy grey toes into the bruised linoleum and crushing coconuts between his bare feet.

Spontaneity is always appreciated when you go out dancing, but if your man keeps snorting like an oil-covered seal, if he has all the grace of a ruptured badger after, of course, he spreads his dance chart all over the floor, offload him. The same holds true for sudden, uncontrollable singing, especially if he sounds like a hog chomping on squash rinds, or a jackrabbit in distress.

Those guys who think it the height of grooviness to avoid taking showers are also an odoriferous drag; these unwashed vegetables are likely to be picked up on a personal-hygiene rap. My secretary, Honeysuckle Moonglow, once fell in love with some dolt who didn't realize he was supposed to bathe regularly until he saw a cat doing it, and now he sits around licking his wrists all day. She now goes with a snob who rubs sand into his scalp to make people think he has a home in Palm Springs.

Perhaps the greatest tip-off to a guy's real personality is his face, so certain features should be carefully examined. For example, if he has a mouth like a letter slot, he's probably great at eating pancakes, but that really doesn't do you any good. The same is true if he has a tiny mouth like a thumbhole in a pot of suet. Avoid him if his ears are so pendulous he can swat flies with them. And if he has a complexion that's so pitted it looks like an abandoned anthill, or as if it's been splattered by shrapnel, avoid that cratered countenance. Tell him so, but be gentle. Look at him with open-eyed frankness and say, "Pablo, when you smile, your face sort of splits in the middle and your eyes disappear into your cheeks like oysters going down for the third time in an oyster stew. And as for your complexion, it'll go thundering down in the annals of acne!"

Eyes are an especially delicate, telling area, particularly if they look like a pair of thoughtful cocktail onions, or if they look like two bubbles in a spirit-level, or if he sits there with his eyes opening and closing slowly like a sick bird, or if his eyes are huddled so close together they look like a pair of cuff-links.

Finally, avoid those guys who have a furtive, scholarly look, like a nuclear scientist who sold a few top secrets, and wind him down if he has authoritative jowls and a cold smile, like a silver plate on a coffin.

Conversely, if he's one of those bland guys who must have been conceived in a pallid moment of listless regret, you'd be better off with some stud whose face is constantly contorted into an expression of concupiscent intensity, and who refers to his wrinkles as "deeply etched souvenirs of hormonal responsibility."

> *To be good is to be noble, but to teach*
> *others how to be good is nobler, and a*
> *lot less trouble.*

Eyes are an especially delicate, telling area, particularly if they look like a pair of thoughtful cocktail onions.

Appearances: For Guys Reconnoitering Girls

The object of this particular exercise is to find you guys the kind of girl who likes to take a tub bath in a motorcycle sidecar on the center divider of the busiest Foreplay Freeway . . . a blithe spirit who can fulfill your wildest fantasies without sending you screaming off to the frenzy farm. My legendary expertise in this area is a matter of codified fact, and stands unchallenged by shrieking, strident, hysterical femlibs. I have no patience with unprofessionalism, so let me now haul off and win your credulity, and help you avoid the kind of girl, who, if she were a little more feminine, could become a lumberjack, a stevedore, or a roller-derby matron.

Make mental notes, men, of first impressions. If she wears brillo-pad dress shields, she's going to be a tough, abrasive babe. Does she look like a test pilot for heavy-duty push-up bras? or does she give you the impression that she has just been named by the Butyl Manufacturers of America, Miss Vulcanized Inner-tube? These things matter, guys, and you better pay attention, or one morning you'll wake up next to someone shooting up estrogen-injected Nujol and stapling up the rips in her tattered, coffee-stained rayon babydolls.

We all have different tastes, but I've found that most guys prefer girls who can make a sweater look like a remarkable example of stress under pressure, rather than a girl who's so tall and skinny her hair looks like a bird's nest on a flagpole and is affectionately known as Captain Kidd because of her sunken chest.

A high-strung woman can get very tiresome, especially when she's standing there all smiley and nervous and rich and giggly and eager and knowing, full of girlish chortles and smirks and nervous twitches as facial tics pursue each other across her palsied features like frightened snipe. On the other hand, those stoned-out zombies aren't any shortcut to happiness either, walking around in the most fashionable hippie slouch, with concave chest and protruding pelvis, in an advanced state of cadaverous charm developed by moulting in malodorous communes, two-in-a-sleeping-bag.

Clothes can give you strong indications of things to come, like a doll in a blazer and bell-bottomed pantsuit with a balloon seat, probably has something to hide. And you can always tell those country girls who went barefoot 'til they were fifteen. When they first put shoes on her, she thought she was caught in some sort of trap and she tried to chew her foot off at the ankle. Clothes can sometimes also contribute to other things, like how she walks with, for example, her clunky thong shoes hooked onto her hip-hazard high-rise.

Definitely beware of Lolitas who are too young to leave their mothers, but are too decorative to be left at home. That kind can go from baby fat to middle-aged spread mighty fast, all smoldering warmth and sleepy-eyed promise, with amber eyes and porcelain-doll complexion; she's cute but deadly, like a lapdog with rabies. In six months you'll be burnt out and gutted like a six-alarm blaze in an old warehouse.

Watch for ominous rumblings from her digestive system, if you get the chance—it may be an incipient peptic ulcer for which you'll suffer—and be careful of girls who are so emotional they cry at untied shoelaces. A little flair for the dramatic is OK, like a bikini of genuine ocelot skin that reveals prospects of a very big and shapely future, but if her hairdo looks as if it's been hit once too often by a sonic boom, forget it. Speaking of hair, if it hangs in lustrous waves over her collarbones, that's fine, but if it's concealing ears which hang in pendulous waves over her well-rounded shoulders, you can probably do better. (My landlady has thick, jet-black glistening hair, but she wears long gloves so it won't show.)

Be alert for women who have had all the bones removed from their faces to give them softer expressions, and women with knees like doorknobs that lead nowhere. What you want is someone between the age of consent and collapse, someone without glazed eyeballs, and that birdlike quality known as crow's feet. Avoid women who wear black crepe garters in memory of those who have passed beyond. You want a girl guaranteed to flip your toggle switch, a girl whose geodesic architecture is beyond anything developed in the dome of Buckminster Fuller; you want a girl who is self-reliant: If she can't afford a bidet, she does a handstand in her shower. Avoid those women who are described to you as "not exactly beautiful, but not quite ugly, either." That means she's like tapioca pudding: Nice, but unexciting, and maybe a little lumpy. What's worse, though, is the kind who "has a type of beauty all her own." That means her face looks as if some medieval master had sculpted it out of fine clay and then dropped it while it was still wet.

There are some little personal traits that can be noticed immediately, like if the girl you're looking at smears on so much lipstick she looks like a Ubangi who's just discovered strawberry jam, you can usually assume that she likes the lavish approach, and probably has the glands of a champion; then, when you go to her apartment and see that the towels are marked "Hers" and "Transient" you know she's probably overdone it. She tends to yawn at both ends.

I have a theory that a woman's beauty is more the result of how she makes up her mind than how she makes up her face—unless, of course, without her makeup she looks like an unfurnished room. And always check her superstitions; to some girls a four-leaf clover means a forthcoming marriage; to others it means good luck.

Some women suffer from what I call the burden of beauty, and they are really in a sad situation. Many beautiful women never develop their inner resources because men seem to be satisfied with their exteriors; these women are caged in luscious bodies that always betray them into the arms of the wrong kind of men. The most successful woman is a beauty who conducts her life as if she were plain; if she does this, she won't fall into the eternal trap best stated in Ballance's Law of Traumatized Attraction: The beautiful woman has a frantic battle with time because people never forgive her for growing old; it makes them feel sad, as when a rose fades and withers away.

The tone of a girl's voice can let you know a lot about her attitude, especially if there's a lot of accumulated, pent-up resentment in it, drenched in disenchantment. And beware the girl whose finishing-school accent suggests she has been edu-cated, inadequately, at Uppity-Puppity Tech. Ballance's Laryn-geal Law states that a woman speaks with her lips to *explain,* and with her throat to *convince.*

Whether your girl has tulip tonsils or a voice rated RR for Raspy Raunchiness, whether she lies a lot in a frothy soft beige contralto that's always foaming on the rocks of accuracy, whether she has a drawl that comes straight up from a secret compartment in her pantyhose, or whether she projects a chilly tone like a breeze off the freezing tundra, *listen* to her, Pal, listen intently to what she says and what she doesn't say. Study those pauses, that delicate catch in her pipes as she pits her mind against your pitted mind, monitor those vocal nuances and you'll be able to anticipate and capture womankind's most evanescent moods and humors. You will unlock the mysteries of a woman's mind, you will probe the innermost reaches of the female universe.

The same girl can have eyes to match her car (crosseyed Chrysler, bloodshot Buick), or her eyes can be shifty and opaque, and give you an overwhelming compulsion to say, "Honey, I wish your eyes were closer to mine instead of so close together."

Do her eyes brim with invitation like haunting pools of promise, or is she just nearsighted? Are those blank eyes a mirror of her innocence or are they bland and round and as expressionless as Raggedy Ann's? Do her drug-disoriented eyes spin like slow pinwheels, or are her eyes like two righteous raisins stuck in a pudding of utter contempt? Do her eyes make restless remarks because of her nervous habit of detaching her own retinas? Does she have cool, emancipated eyes or is she all hot-eyed and uncomprehending? Are her eyes dark like melting Milk Duds? or is there a man-wanted sign in her hash-brown eyes? Do her eyes project a penetrating and skeptical intelligence? or does she carouse so much her eyeballs are the color of crimson geraniums? Does she have big, shiny, compelling eyes or does she have a reproachful reptilian gaze set in a baleful countenance? Does she have cold, anthracite eyes or do her eyes shimmer like crushed velvet? Is she always blinking her luminous eyes under a canopy of false eyelashes, rolling them heartlessly in their pearl-handled sockets? When you take her in your spindly arms, do her tiny, orangutan eyes glitter with delight? When she looks at you, are her large, moist eyes filled with love? When she's miffed at you, does she give you the old "geological survey," otherwise known as a stony stare? Well, Sport, never forget that the human eye is an undullable tale-teller, and the woman to avoid at all costs is the one with a disconcerting buzz in her eyes, a wild glaze, a crazy glare—an optical effect which, if detected in a *horse*—well, no one would ever bet on it. So consider yourself warned. And remember Ballance's Opthalmological Law: Heredity determines the color of your eyes, but love lights them up. Now if you'll excuse me a moment—there's a humming-bird caught under my left contact lens, and he's trying to peck his way out.

If your girl is so bowlegged she can tune in the TV set without blocking your view, if she has knuckles the size of walnuts and eyeballs and teeth of glistening pink in what seems to be a terrifying combination of conjunctivitis and trench mouth, don't fling her out of your life for she may be the only girl you'll ever know who walks as if she's wearing leopard skin underpants with a secret compartment for her solid-state circuitry and most lovable component parts. Be alert for that lovely little thing frugging around, spraying charm out of every enlarged pore, because she's about to ask for spare change. Soft hands require hard cash.

Avoid round-faced farm girls, their sturdy features already setting into placid no-nonsense domesticity; and, remember, a woman doesn't have to be an athlete to smell like one. I knew one who always smelled like fifteen minutes of brisk basketball.

But I didn't mind too much . . . she always gave me plenty of free throws.

Beware of hidden helpers, too, you guys, like the girl who always gives you the impression of eternal youth just might be cheating. She could be wearing tucks behind her ears, instead of perfume. But all of us prefer the kind of girl who requires eyeball-recapping if you gaze at her too long, rather than a girl with hips spread out like a beach umbrella, who needs a heavy-duty girdle to squeeze into a kimono, and is so fat that when she falls down she rocks herself to sleep trying to get up. The kind of girl who overeats is the kind of girl who could help herself more by helping herself less. She has no glandular problem—she just suffers from an overactive spoon. These very large girls usually get their looks from their mothers, who were sandhogs. While it's true that you don't want to fool around with a girl who's lost so much weight that she looks like a crankshaft—one who stands out like a razorback hog at a livestock show—you still wouldn't want to make it with a doll whose chin is all lard and looks like a Victorian cushion sewn to her collarbone. If she looks as if she were force-fed on pasta, fork-lift her out of your life.

A sweat hog, incidentally, is an overage porker with absolutely no redeeming traits, a skin-covered blimp, suffering from rampaging elephantiasis, the kind of woman you have to trundle around in a wheelbarrow, with so much fat on her face that a plastic surgeon lifting it would just remove her ears, and stick on handles. Say to her, "Honey, I'd tear my heart out for you if I had a pair of tweezers."

Watch out for those girls who walk as if they're churning butter, especially if they're into Yoga, because when she gets into a lotus position, meditating all over the floor, her legs are bound to lock up on her, and unless you're a fireman, you'll never get her unknotted. She's a compulsive contortionist and not for you, Pal.

Girls who study ballet are usually limber and supple, with a tantalizing tuck-under walk, and the one I knew would have

She has no glandular problem, she just suffers from an over-active spoon.

been a star except that every time she stood on her toes, her arches collapsed. By the way, a girl who's a dog but who can dance great . . . well, it's like putting an Elgin movement into a Mickey Mouse watch.

Try to avoid dogs if you can; you know, real woofers, the kind who are so doggy they give you rabies. Both extremes are bad: The kind who are so thin that if they put on blonde wigs, they'd look like dandelions, and the kind who are fat in places where other women don't even *have* places. The same holds true for those women who have had their faces lifted so many times the only expression they have left is a trancelike look of appalled disbelief. And you've seen those brown and withered ladies who look like old leather bottles left out in the sun for two weeks, with the cork out. Avoid them; even their eyeballs get wrinkled.

What most of us like are women who can grind their galvanic hips and make osteopathic history when they dance with us, but stay away from emaciated and scrawny creatures who hate to wear bras; their sawtooth shoulder blades hack up the straps and they can't shoulder their responsibilities.

Most guys are usually confronted with some kind of choice, so choose carefully. Don't wind up with 180 pounds of neurotic scrap iron exuding bogus charm, when you can have a lovely, dainty little thing who looks like a sensitive and highly intelligent polliwog.

Sometimes a girl's appearance can handicap her work-life, so if you guys are counting on the extra income, be sure your girl doesn't have buck teeth . . . if you got her a job as a bubble-dancer, her career would blow up in her face.

Sometimes a woman attributes her youthful appearance to sleeping with the windows open, eating green leafies, and trick lighting. Still it remains a clear hint that something is amiss if everytime she yawns, her ears disappear, because she has a mouth like a torn pocket; far better is a woman whose mouth is so tiny that when she eats a jellybean, she has to cram it in with a shoehorn. On the other hand, she *could* have a mouth so big that it takes her an hour to put on lipstick, and she has to do it with a mop. Call her "Amazon" because she's so wide at the mouth. Her lips might be so large and loose that instead of buttering her bread, she just butters her lips and slides the slices in. Her tongue is so long, she can seal a letter after it's in the mailbox.

Ballance's Labial Law emphasizes that mouths mean much; you know what I mean, buddy, she fights and bites and then suddenly melts in hot surrender . . . her proud, sensual mouth bares away from her glistening teeth in a snarl of desire and then, afterward, that same mouth *softens* into a half-pout of loving slavery. But if her mouth is so big that when she smiles she gets lipstick on her ears; if her mouth has hideous lips, all thick and wet and crimson, if she has a mouth like a split watermelon, big enough to sing a duet as she breathes hot licorice in your face, you can have her. All of a sudden I remember the first girl I hung my fraternity pin (Beta Theta Pi) on. She had a huge, sagging lower lip. But I didn't mind because her upper lip covered it.

Once in a while a face lift helps, especially if it puts her mouth above her chin. Otherwise she might have gone on looking like something that Ringling Brothers were saving for a bad year, low center of gravity and all, complexion irrevocably clashing with the wallpaper. You can tell when everything goes wrong, though, especially when the only way she could coordinate her outfit would be to put her shoes on the wrong feet.

Every man enjoys a hyperpassionate girl, but it is usually prudent to notice if she is digging her fingernails into your wallet, leaving costly love scratches. Personally, I like nice soft hands, especially if they feel like a couple of warm slices of calves' liver. I always watch for a calloused thumb, however, because I don't want to get involved with a girl who's done so much hitchhiking she's showing up on roadmaps.

Legs are another favorite diversion, so I hate to see a girl so knock-kneed that she can't even get dental floss between them, the sort of girl who has to jack her legs apart to get her pantyhose on. That kind of girl can wind up looking as if she got up in the morning on the wrong side of her slab. Fat legs,

legs that look as if she has them on upside-down, just are not acceptable. These lardos can only buy one thing ready-made, and that's a shower curtain; they don't have measurements anymore, just time zones.

I once knew a flaky girl who had such an infallible homing instinct she never got lost. She just followed her own dandruff back home. This same beauty had the baritone of a detention-home matron, and was sort of chubby. In a green dress, she looked like a bloated grasshopper. She was the kind of girl who should have been mercifully put to sleep, snuffed out before her first candle, so I'm certainly grateful that she turned down my piteous proposal of marriage.

I like a girl who wears ultra-lowcut hip-huggers, the type of girl who offers to the world her aggressive navel, glaring at the world like an eyeless socket. Expensive girls can be appealing, but love is a money-spending thing. I know one doll who wears a lot of jewelry, for example. She glistens and glitters like a chopped-up rainbow, wearing gigantic diamond rings with stones the size of locomotive headlights. That's only her sports jewelry, by the way, and she insists that money is like a sixth sense; without it, you can't really enjoy the other five.

Despite the obvious economic overhead, this kind of girl can often be a better deal than a real ecology freak who loves Nature, despite what it did to her. Or a waterlogged waif who wears a false beard and hangs around with surfers at Zuma beach. Or a lady who caps her own teeth, likes to lie in bed under a sunlamp, and makes toast on her own chest. It's always intimidating to be walking down the street with a girl and see someone point at her and say, "I've seen better shapes fall out of ice cream cones!"

Better to go with an ex-cheerleader who still has a nice set of pompoms, even if she does contrive her powerful bra straps from old booster cables. Do yourself a favor, though, and stay away from those older debutantes, those weather-beaten in-genues with an accent as thick as their ankles, and a dowager's hump for a figure. Those babes wear ponytails where the ponies wear them; they've not only *kept* their girlish figures, they've *tripled* them. Unless you yearn to be a missionary in the field of fat, clear out, Pal, go over the side without a ripple.

Incidentally, avoid the hyperkinetic type, too. You know, the kind who are so nervous and high-strung that they can thread a sewing machine while it's in motion, coming at you with a grotesque smile and a lurching curtsy after being picked up for rolling winos and brawling with sailors in a seafront bar.

When confronted with the extremes, it is my recommendation that you opt for the girl with hands just like her mother's; small and delicate, with long slender fingers. Even though these hands may slide easily into a man's wallet, it's better than a Clydesdale Cleopatra with her great, quivering, pudding thighs. It's also better than a hard, trim, professionally pretty airline stewardess, the kind of chick who is mechanically sexy, and more in love with looking attractive than actually being attractive. That flashing-white-teeth-dark-brown-eye innuendo is usually just put on with the rest of her lavish makeup. With them, you're dealing with strictly automatic penny-in-the-slot charm. She's a city-bred, coin-fed girl who will pop the lugnuts off your wire wheels, then disappear without a trace.

> *A woman is never overweight until*
> *she has run out of places to hide it.*

Attitudes—A Question of Style I

A Filly's Guide to Studs

This is a guide for you fillies, an effort to help you avoid the kind of guy who looks good on the outside, but is rotten on the inside. He might just be an innocuous clod, a harmless human cipher, a rimless zero, but don't associate with him for he will be unflattering to your image of yourself, which, by the way, is mighty important. So these are telling little tips on how to spot a vacuous vaquero, the stud who is all wrangler in the saddle, but all horse between the temples. He might be fine, that palomino Percheron, standing there nibbling num-nums out of your hand, but marry him and you'll come a-cropper.

Then there's the guy who is master of the inappropriate word, whose life is a triumph of fantasy over realism, who sleeps in a nest of shredded Tarot cards, and goes around humming that Yuletide tango, "While Shepherds Washed Their Socks by Night." He usually comes from a town so small that for excitement they go down to the used-car lot and watch the chrome rust. On Saturday night his idea of a fling is to race down to the gas station and watch the attendant check dipsticks.

This clod has lots of background for failure, too; his father usually arrives in the US a penniless immigrant, and in only five years he becomes a penniless citizen. He usually thinks he's an ultra-urbane guy, urbanity being his hobby, and he thinks he easily qualifies as captain of the All-American Suave Team while, in point of fact, he's the biggest suave in town.

Perhaps you find yourself with a guy who, despite a gruff, outspoken manner, is really very harsh and abrasive. This is usually the type that started out as an infant prodigy. However, he continued to be an infant long after he ceased to be a prodigy. These creeps have a deadly flair for stirring amorous animosity, so keep alert.

Girls, don't be so easily conned. Before you worship the ground a guy walks on, be sure he owns it first. You may wind up with a one-man leper colony, and trying to rely on a guy like that is like leaning on a broken crutch.

Some men just seem to have an infinite capacity for treachery, so when you meet a smooth operator, it is wise to keep the possibility of rotten character flaws in the back of your mind. These renegade Romeos will try to find the way to your heart on devious back roads, and if they make it, your affections will be heartlessly squandered. Save your passion for someone more deserving, someone like, well, me.

Sometimes you get lucky, though, and you can tell immediately that this is the kind of guy who never knows what day it is anymore, since he started bathing regularly. Or his dialogue is evasive, the point of his conversation being as elusive as a ferret in a conduit factory.

You can really tell what kind of attitude a guy has about you by the kind of movies he takes you to. If, for example, he insists on a family-type picture, that's perfectly OK, unless, of course it's the Marquis De Sade's family. Watch out for those X-rated films, like *It Happened One Night After Another,* or *Elizabeth and Essex and David and Bathsheba,* or *Bambi, An Authentic Stag Film.* Musical comedies can be charming, like *Tora, Tora, Tora,* with tap-dancing Kamakaze pilots. Another type of movie that is always entertaining and speaks well of your man would be the intricate-plot film, in which Jane Fonda is chased through the Canadian Northwest by a crazed Mountie who's been shooting up prewar Preparation H. But by all means flee in terror from the guy who says: "I don't want to see any more incest, rape, or adultery in movies. I get enough of that at home."

Some guys have about as much polish as a pair of tennis shoes, while others are crazy about anything antique: Lovers, furniture, cars, wallpaper, and political concepts. Many men drink a lot, but are actually some of the nicest guys on two feet—if they could only stay on them. If your guy is a lush, remember that alcoholics usually have an ego about as frail as a moth's wings. Tread gently on his head, and lovingly on his heart and giblets.

A few men are such hypochondriacs that they think freckles are contagious, and these guys are usually so negative that when they hold a sea shell to their ears, instead of the romantic roar of the surf, all they hear is a faucet dripping. These guys can be pure poison, with the eyes of a child and the mind of a Borgia. Communication can become a trifle difficult, sort of like eating a pound of day-old Cream of Wheat out of a cracked earthenware bowl. It's really futile, like trying to control the wind by jamming the weather vane.

Another aggravating type is the unstable man who is always poised between a cliché and an indiscretion. Going with him is like living with a ticking time bomb.

Then there's the guy who moves through life with all the grace and charm of a bull with eight bandarillos hooked into his back muscles. This is the diesel-operated dullard with a reptilian reputation who leaves a trail of bouncing checks and broken hearts. This is the guy who would put a knife in your back and then have you arrested for carrying a concealed weapon.

Take care not to get too heavily involved with the man who is crazed with avarice, always hustling a buck, always eager to pounce on a penny like a duck on a June bug. This guy will leave you wallowing around in perpetual melancholy, because while he's hustling he also becomes ambidextrous, able to brush aside a dinner check with either hand.

Don't ignore these Ballancean warning signals, girls; remember the deckhand who said to the skipper of the Titanic: "Captain, I think something might be wrong; my sox are getting wet." Still, if his only problem is shyness, it could come from his strict upbringing. After all, I didn't even look under a car hood until I was twenty-three. What ever you do, don't compromise. Never make excuses for a fat slob with gross gelatinous hippo loins by murmuring, "He's a fascinating guy, for his age and weight and I call him my great Tub of Love!" Let him waddle out of your life like a web-footed panda.

Try to avoid the kind of personality that makes instant enemies at friendship clubs, the kind of frenetic person who is so industrious that when he has nothing else to do he sits around and knits his brows with his thumb up his toga. If he's not sulking, he's being aggressively silent, even though he's a charter member of the Feel-No-Pain Society and is chronically snockered. If you have one of those constant meddlers, one of those spies of life who is suffocatingly close and revoltingly neighborly, dump him. It might be like insulting a shark circling a leaky lifeboat, ready to dart in with a flank attack, but I'll protect you. Follow all of my piercing precepts and one day you'll be carried triumphantly from the field on the shoulders of your admirers, one of whom will be me.

Another type is the intensely sincere bore, a guy with a flair for conspiracy, a tantalizing, tormented talent for intrigue. This is a lad who is not even worth his weight in Librium, whose vocabulary is small, but the turnover is terrific. The kind of guy who was born stupid and had a relapse.

Insecure guys can drive you up a wall every time without fail; and that's their only consistency. I know one guy who gave up his psychotherapist because he found out the good doctor also lived with his mother, chewed his nails, and told fortunes on the side. These guys drive so many women into nervous breakdowns that they get royalties from psychiatrists. With a heart of basic black and the articulation quotient of a 50-cent parakeet, this Lothario is an incessant loser.

Heredity can influence your guy's outlook on things, my dear, so back off when he brags that he was his mother's only *legitimate* son. He's as mixed up as a chicken that hatched in an egg beater. Getting through to him could be tougher than a night in the drunk tank. He could just be one of those uncomplaining men without any authority, to whom things always happen catastrophically.

If your guy is not exactly under the weather but clouding up fast, he could be going through a change of venue, playing the ancient caper, the eternal love-gamesmanship of amorous advance and inviting retreat. But then, again, perhaps he's just worried because his conversation is a treasure trove of excruciating banalities, and he can't get anywhere because he has no focus, he fritters time away, he's the sort of aimless oaf who lectures on navigation while the ship is foundering on the rocks.

This guy may not be mature, but he certainly is callow. He likes to talk to strangers about friends who will soon become enemies, for he harbors all the emotions of a divided amoeba. But immaturity can be cured with a little experience, which reminds me of when I was very shy, back in high school, and I was dating an eager girl with whom I yearned to lock braces. Up until this time we just used to sit around and watch each other's face break out. I think it was about our tenth date, and we were sitting on the couch in her front room when suddenly she reached over and snapped off the light. I could take a hint; I realized she was trying to tell me something. So I was understanding and cooperative, and gentlemanly; I knew she was trying to tell me goodnight so I got up and went home.

Other guys act as if they just graduated Magna Cum Laude in Manipulation, whereas most of the time they're so dull that if they slipped into a coma it would be an improvement. Other guys have to be the life of the party so, after some particularly stupid act, suggest that for an encore he go over the Freeway in a barrel. Also, never get serious with a dragster. He spends all week tuning and polishing his car instead of tinkering with, and stroking, his girl.

Some guys always act as if they're overdue for a distemper shot, always wild and impulsive, while others are semi-inventive. Like the guy I know who crossed an intersection with a convertible and got a blonde. She fell for him like an egg from a tall chicken. But toward her, he affects a cavalier flamboyance and the poor, worshipping girl still doesn't realize that if it weren't for his pulmonary emphysema he wouldn't have any personality at all.

Have faith in other human beings, but always cut the cards. Trust people, but always examine the dice.

You probably fantasize about finding a guy who will think of you every waking moment, but you'd better figure out how much of his day that comprises. Of course this slug-a-bed could have an occasional fleeting redeeming trait, perhaps a carefully honed instinct for survival. You may well admire the way he struggles back on his feet everytime he goes bankrupt, but aren't you getting a little weary of living off factory-second potato chips, and day-old gopher loaf?

Never get involved with any pipsqueak whose eyes are aglow with harebrained plans, a simpleton who is full of get-poor-quick schemes. He's always clutching a stack of credit cards, which means only that he's in hock to his own image of himself.

These are the disaster-prone types who get injured and carried off the field while trying out for the debating team; they have to pluck him out of the turf with a nut pick.

Find an opportunist, a guy who keeps his weather eye out for the main chance, and avoid the man who is hobbled by excessive prudence. Say, for example, he buys something for one dollar and sells it for two dollars. He gives you a grin of snaggle-toothed affability and remarks, "I make my one percent and I'm satisfied."

Don't ever get too compassionate or you'll come down with a nasty case of humane poisoning, especially if you're playing around with a guy whose brains seem to be, well, limited. Avoid men who wallow in ruinous, wild, and negative behavior, because it is totally self-destructive, and steer clear of those dimwits who've won the Nobel Prize in knuckleheadedness.

Those guys with voices like birds and bodies to match, are usually victims of first-cousin breeding; so check his genealogy gingerly—the best part of his family tree is probably underground. I ache for you girls to become everything you are capable of becoming, not just a cupcake who assumes she's on earth merely to pamper some posturing, preening dandy.

If your guy is aimless and befuddled, seething with residual irascibility, if he acts like a man from Mars assigned to the wrong planet, just remember that consigning yourself to him is like hitching a racehorse to a plow.

So don't bother with guys whose idea of a big evening is to sit at home watching his parakeet moult; this guy's imagination soars from minuscule to tiny, spreading a pall of placidity as it inches through his sodden cerebellum. He wants to do his own thinking, but he doesn't know how. Examine your situation carefully; if it's like one of those hidden-figure problems in a child's picture puzzle, ask yourself how many animals can you find, and are they predatory carnivorous bipeds?

If you're miffed at your boyfriend, what you say is, "It sure is a rat race around here, and believe me, I know the perfect cast for it." If your guy comes home and flings himself on the couch and you're getting tired of it, what you do is turn that

If your guy comes home and flings himself on the couch and you're tired of it, what you do is turn that couch upside down and put a sign on it in large block letters, reading: "Out Of Order."

couch upside down and put a sign on it, in large block letters, reading: "Out of Order."

If there's an unstable quality to your man, like nitro-glycerine, or if he's so dull they're naming a butter knife after him, it's exit time. Still, remember when confronted with new and better possibilities, it is more fun to have shared a small foreign car than never to have loved at all.

> *Power is the ability to make people do what*
> *they don't want to do.*

Attitudes—A Question of Style II

A Stud's Guide to Fillies

Basically, what we're all after is a woman with sex appeal. What is sex appeal? Well, the guidelines generally apply to both men and women, because people with sex appeal make you feel alive and show a genuine interest in you as a person; they have the ability to get out of themselves, and can make another person feel appreciated as attractive and worthy. By giving the appearance of completeness and wholeness, of self-confidence and contentment, they finally help others to simply feel good about themselves. Sex appeal is the art of giving; flirting is the art of making a girl feel pleased with herself.

This doesn't necessarily mean you should find a girl who is so softhearted that she won't even eat an egg for breakfast until she finds out if the hen pulled through all right, and won't eat a Popsicle because she's afraid of hurting it; who's so sensitive that she takes a bad sunset personally. Put her at ease by letting her touch you in an intimate place—your wallet.

Avoid girls who like to read murder mysteries every night while playing Bach on a flute, and those very scholarly subdebs who spend their time wondering if Santa Claus lives at the geographical or the magnetic North Pole. Still, if she carries a 40-horsepower vibrator, complete with twelve exotic bolt-on attachments, you might reconsider.

Men, it is important to find a contemporary woman, a girl who understands that the new dilemma is how to balance the security of love and marriage with the mobility of freedom and achievement. You should always be understanding, especially if she has a voice that sounds as if she's had her vocal chords replaced with pussy willows.

Some women are easy to impress, especially if they come from a town so small that the height of their cultural season is the arrival of a singing telegram. Other women see themselves as ultra-chic, and are harder to deal with; like the honey that carries her pills in a Pucci shoulder-holster, sitting there sipping Midol martinis and picking like an anxious raccoon at her oleander salad with surgical dressing. Sometimes the only reason an ultra-chic girl like that—worn to a frazzle by jet lag—hasn't broken all ten commandments is that she doesn't know how to make graven images.

No sense blowing it on a slob, though, the kind of sweetie who likes to shuffle around in her hobnailed thongs, listening to her resonant digestion, anxiously monitoring embolisms churning through her great aorta. She's the type who'll be named honorary inspector of hides and ticks by the Tijuana International Border Patrol, Ladies Auxiliary. She usually lives with one guy after another, in rapid succession, a sort of sequential monogamy which would work better if she wore sequential taillights. Her voice will sound as if she's been blowing on both ends of a sour pitchpipe, and her obstinacy would be equal to her folly, if her folly were equal to her inanity. This winner has a heart of gold and a head of lead, so don't even consider her; I mean after all, one girl with five illegitimate children, a sort of amorous turnstile, isn't quite the calm and equable type you're searching for.

There are many stunt women in the field of emotions, and

you know you're up against one if you have about as much control over her as you'd have over a bucket of mercury tossed down a marble staircase. If she is so polished that everything she says is a reflection on someone else, if her idea of generosity is to keep nothing to herself, well, she's just plain unstable, spraying chlorine on her hair to make people think she has a swimming pool one minute, and the next minute putting anchovy paste behind her ears because she loves the sea; she has the touch of a starving cobra and you guys would be better off making like a mongoose.

If your girl is petulant and tantrum-prone, perhaps she's just cold-blooded (a mosquito bit a vexed maiden I once knew and the poor bug died instantly of pneumonia), or she could prefer men who go for the more refined things in life, like oil, and she sees you as strictly reclaimed leftovers. Face it, sport, a girl is rarely a paragon of prudery for nothing. Of course she could, on the other hand, wear outfits so sexy she can only send them to a mature dry cleaner. She could also charm the birds down from the trees and, once she's got them down on the ground, she just might gobble them up and do the same to you.

I once met an enchantress who had a photographic mind, but unfortunately, there wasn't any film in the camera. She had a highly volatile volcanic personality; in fact, that hole in her head was probably so she could let off steam. Still, she did look kind of neat, standing there snapping her garters, all surly and sultry. She was more fun than a barrel of monkeys. Not as pretty, perhaps, but a lot more fun.

Plenty of women are so fast with their mouths that the only thing that can cheat them out of the last word is an echo. That same babe can be famous for her gentle wit and hard drinking, but don't let her make you feel as if you're a certified kink, ready for custodial care at Addled Acres just because she started her hopechest thirty years ago with a tablecloth, and has built it up into a hotel-sized linen wardrobe. She's the one with problems, pal.

Face it, not all girls are equally entertaining. Most guys feel that charm is something possessed by girls with luscious figures.

I don't agree—some of these dear things are so phony that they can't even say hello without choreography, and they are usually remembered for their tiny, bird-seed intellect. They are partial women with a halfway heart.

I knew another girl who had plateaued at a level of dynamic mediocrity; she was so cautious she got vaccinated when she went to a foreign movie. She was somewhat reserved and virginal; if she had been the chaperone with Adam and Eve, there'd have been no world. That kind of girl, I discovered, thrives on anguish and remorse. She kept a jar of grief on the shelf like jam and took some every day to keep going, to sustain her malaise.

Some cuties always remain calm and smiling, no matter what happens, like a hospital floor-nurse in the presence of a terminal disease or a fatal wound. But watch out when they cut loose, chum, because this same cool captivator will wind up sounding like she lost her duenna at a bullfight.

Find a girl who not only loves to go to the movies, but goes to the movies to love. But try to circumnavigate those conservative girls who like to return home with the same lipstick they started out with. That is an authentic super-bummer.

The girl who flatly refuses to kiss a man who has whiskey on his breath is usually waiting for a man with champagne on his breath. This is the straightforward type who often forgets that a woman is charming until she begins to rely on it to pull her through all situations. She can also be coy, and somewhat modest, always pulling down the shade when she takes off her see-through blouse and puts on an invisible bra.

The girl who is always making helpful suggestions is probably worse, though, like one I know who was undergoing psychoanalysis, for example. She was spreadeagled on his Naugahyde couch and she told the psychiatrist that his ceiling could certainly stand some painting. This same girl was also the very soul of discretion. Even when she entered a revolving door, she was careful in choosing the people she went around with.

Let's not get involved with a conventional girl, either. You know, the kind who follow all the conventions. These women of mystery, these double-dipped enigmas get more than a little garish when they start charging for their services; "twice the vice at half the price" is her slogan. She can be a highbrow girl with low-cut ideas, or she could be so good and gentle she wouldn't step on a saber-toothed boll weevil. It's that slight speech impediment you have to watch out for, the inability to say "no."

Sometimes you run into a woman who is such a snob that she ought to have plastic surgery to have her nose lowered. Sometimes she can have latent playgirl tendencies, but she'll arouse every feeling except trust. If trying to follow her lah-de-dah reasoning is like trying to ride a hockey puck, and she has all the personality of a vulture with carbuncles, you might as well write her off. That voice full of bogus cultivation and synthetic finishing-school drawl, complete with hauteur and repressed noblesse oblige, restricts her to Cluck City.

The right girl will accelerate a man's ascent and increase his candlepower, even if he keeps her busier than a bubbledancer at a dart-throwers convention. She might be colder than the knees of a walrus to others, but watch her chortle like a well-disposed percolator when you ask, "Can a girl who has a mole be happy with a gopher?" and she retorts, "Yes, if their teeth match."

It is not wise to get involved with an unfrocked hustler who has seen more love than a policeman's flashlight. Trying to get through to her will be like trying to squeeze bread through a keyhole, and even though she's probably used to fending for herself, she's all signpost and no destination. You'll end up going around in circles, like a fly with a broken wing.

Remember, chums, that only good girls keep diaries, because bad girls don't have time, even if they are dainty and fastidious (I once knew a charming little minx who would go all over her bawdy bod with a Q-tip soaked in cucumber brine). Keep your conversation moving, guys, and notice if a girl's attention span peaks out at four seconds. If it does, Bombsville.

When the love-light starts shining through her eyes, pal, make sure it's not from a hole in the back of her head and, if she's an explosive girl, remember that living with her would be like laying a bangalore torpedo across the barbed-wire entanglements of amour.

Guys, there are more important things in life than money, but they won't go out with you if you don't have any. I remember a real schemer I once dated; a clever and conniving girl, but she was frank and honest about it. She said, "Bill, if you really love me, you'll write me a packet of compromising letters I can save and use against you when it's all over." At least she was considerate, like those women who learn to weave so they can take walks with their heavy-drinking lovers down stupefaction lane. Still, the best way to soften a girl up is to marinate her in money.

If you really want to impress a new girl, take her out to eat at a fancy restaurant. If you have any doubts about the place, they will immediately be dispelled if you ask for a glass of water, and the waiter asks you, "What year, sir?" Anyway, you'll be able to gauge your success or failure by casually noticing the little things your date does. If she lifts her dress and shamelessly scratches her appendectomy scar, you know you're in trouble. She's "DOA"—Dog on Arrival.

But guys, never turn down a date because you think she's too old for you. Remember, a man can get a lot of great tunes out of an old accordian, if he knows just how to squeeze it. If she has a few hashmarks on her thorax, you can refer to your vintage inamorata and her antique ardor in this hip manner: "She's an old girl with a new wrinkle!"

Watch out for that girl whose moods range every twenty seconds from infantile timidity to savage spike-biting irritability, until, of course, something behind her dark eyes goes "ding" and a cash drawer slides open in her greedy mind. Speaking of her mind, it is probably a polar night of icy darkness and hardness, and her remarks are like ammonia: They clear the air but they're not very endearing.

It would also benefit you to avoid a chick who gets mad at you because you clash with the drapes in her moldering VW van. I once knew a beautiful girl of Norwegian registry, who was built especially for navigation in icy waters. In fact, I believe certain chilled explorers named her Miss Polar Circle. Anyway, she was so cold she used to feed poisoned Gainesburgers to seeing-eye dogs; she invented Kelvinator hot pants for frigid women.

Better to find a Seventh Day Adventuress, the kind of doll-baby who won't let anyone make her feel intimidated or diminished. Someone who never allows anyone to rob her of her self-respect and personal sovereignty. This is the girl who will neither lacerate with, nor be lacerated by, snubs. I don't mean to say that you should seek out a subdued little creature quieter than two mice frugging on a blotter.

Or a girl who is hyper-naive (she thinks Mutual Orgasm is an insurance company in Omaha), or a girl who cries a lot (high annual tearfall), or an honor graduate of Epoxy State College, where she majored in adhesiveness.

Avoid teenage girls at all cost; they prefer that shaggy-haired box boy at the neighborhood supermarkup. Psychiatrists report that the long-hair craze is a desire by the young for over-identification with their mothers—which means there's a fortune for someone who can design a guitar with a pacifier, so they can suck and pluck at the same time.

And of course ignore any girl who sits around pensively licking her braids, playing bass ukelele, and getting turned on by the way the neighborhood butcher swings his cleaver and slams it into that slab of beef; she will really create havoc in your sealed-beam, vacuum-packed head.

So, it is best to avoid teeners, and also prudes. I once dated a girl who got her start in showbiz as founder of the Furious Committee to Put a Bra on Little Orphan Annie. It didn't last. What you want instead is a hyper-smart girl, one who closes her eyes while being kissed, but really opens her boyfriend's eyes. Forget the crows, the ones who are so homely that at Christmas time, they kiss the mistletoe and hang her. The same desperate dog will list her lovers in her bogus fantasy-diary under a section labeled "body count."

If you find that certain someone, and you are deliriously happy but it flops as an affair, just follow my own good example: A girl I had the scorchies for went her own way after we quarreled. I decided to forget her, so with a tremendous exertion of will, I did; except for lying awake for five nights and staying indoors waiting for the phone to ring to turn down her quavering apology, which never came.

Men never flash dimples
At girls with big pimples.

Etiquette: What to Do, When and Why

There are a few items of etiquette which can be specifically spelled out like laws, but most of it is derived from basic experience. Like the time I took a lovely girl out to dinner, and her table manners weren't really too swift. She liked to eat with her hands, which didn't bother me until she came to the soup. I felt that she had committed a serious social miscue, but being a true gentleman, I courteously offered her some butter for her singed palms.

Etiquette is simply a means of dealing with and responding to the ceremonies of life, most of which are errors. I will deal with the most important ones, carefully directing my attention to introductions, gifts, generalized behavior and ways to cope with certain disasters, like falling down on a dance floor (just lie there and pretend you've fainted). With this useful knowledge you should be able to handle even most crucial situations without punching the Fail-Safe button.

Introductions are of preeminent importance, especially for you studs out there longing to make a dynamic first impression on some voluptuous gyrator who has caught your roving eye and is mesmerizing you beyond recognition. You could work your way through that panting crowd of admirers, sidle up to her and whisper: "Meet me in an hour and I'll rotate your tires." If she doesn't respond, gaze pensively out the window, and impress her with your neointellectuality; if she asks what you're thinking about, hit her with a mathematical zinger, like "Oh, pardon me, I was just measuring the distance from here to the horizon with my mental compass, hoping to haul my azimuth that way soon with the you at my side."

If this fails, and she still doesn't know who you are, try the sensitive approach: "My dear, you are a blank check in my emotions, and you may fill it out for any amount you wish." If you're still invisible after all that, try this snappy intro: "My darling, let's put out the light and eat the bulb," or, "Extend your swanlike neck, sweetheart, and allow me to plant a glowing, semipermanent kissing hickey on same." Or you can snap your gnarled fingers and come on hip—"Hey, baby, turn out the light and be beautiful."

If you absolutely cannot control yourself, try this humble approach: "Forgive me for stroking you and fondling you, and tapping you, my dear, I thought you were a *statue*. I never knew such beauty existed in *human* form." Friendly threats are often useful if you employ the proper phraseology: "If you fail to go the distance, my love, I'll race out to your house and eviscerate your hibiscus."

By now she's probably wondering if you've flipped your yogurt, but do not relent: "Shall we step into another world and speak of brighter things?" is always a suave query, particularly if preceded by something groveling and banal, like: "Without you, my existence is starved and trivial." Keep her in suspense by smiting your ever-heightening brow and panting, "I think I'm about to undergo a profound emotional experience." Or you can gasp, "Give me your lips, your eyes, your hair," and if she's my kind of girl she'll mutter, "Leave my ears—I'm expecting a phone call!"

Tell her subtly, "Meet me in the henhouse and I'll try to egg you on," because then she'll know that you're quasi-literate. Whether she'll care or not is entirely another matter. Be romantic, and say, "My sweet, didn't we meet in some other hallucination?" and then clinch it by saying, "We'd better be more careful or our love could drag on for years."

If she expresses any doubt, tell her: "Meet me under the rose trellis and I'll spray your fungus, I'll pluck the aphids off your forget-me-nots." If she demurs, become insistent, saying, "Be my girl, tell me you're mine (waving a scrap of paper in her face), and make me tear up this suicide note." If you are forced to leave, or worse yet, are ejected from the premises, just casually utter: "Keep your burners on simmer, 'cause I'll be right back." If she loudly begins to protest your behavior, simply say: "Let me silence you with a primordial kiss on those sensationally pneumatic, Quaker Puffed lips."

The worst possible thing that can happen is she'll start to scream, whereupon you comfort her by saying, "I think I just heard a tiny grenade of hate explode, and the fragments are ringing and ricocheting around the metallic walls of your dear mind." Quietly ask her if the affair is over: "Does this mark the beginning of a rather precipitous decline in our already hideous relationship?" If she starts shaking her head up and down like one of those dolls on the back ledge of a chopped Chevy, you might feign disaster by saying: "I plan to step out in the corridor and fall on my sword."

Should this charmer look as if she's getting hysterical, just ease her through it by saying, "One false move and I'm yours." If she starts swearing at you in basic Anglo-Saxon expletives, don't be appalled. Shake your head sanctimoniously and say, "Let's have no pious sermonizing; no preaching, please." If she starts to run away, pursue her and yell, "You've really blasted me, sweetheart, it may be only a *flesh* wound, but it goes *clear through.*"

Finally, you might have to admit that she's just not your cup of schnapps. If, by now, she's off on an uncontrollable binge of convulsive sobbing alternated with loud gnashing of gums, offer condolences: "Thank you, love, the feeling is mutilated." Then, with a splendid gesture of reconciliation to her ineptitude, say: "In the ruthless realm of relentless romance, I hereby appoint you rookie of the year." Then stalk out in High Dudgeon, a small town north of here.

Let us now concentrate on gifts, the giving of which can often create some rather perplexing problems. I have many solutions for you here, so try to stay alert, and if you feel the need, it is perfectly permissible to take notes. Just don't send them to me, unless, of course, they are protestations of undying affection and loyalty. Those you can have delivered by Currier, if Ives can't make it.

First of all, it is tedious and tiresome when a girl demands largesse. So, let her know you don't take her too seriously, and, if she insists on a fur, give her an evergreen tree. For you girls who are confronted with a super-jealous man, in a kind of reverse of the situation above, and he carries it to crass extremes, I want you to know that the perfect gift for you is coming soon: A Bill Ballance official skeleton key, guaranteed to fit any known chastity belt. This key is certified to unlock all commercial, standard, or custom-made chastity belts; just one turn and you're free. The belt harmlessly drops around your liberated ankles, you step out and into a new life, howling and prowling in the cool of the evening, emotionally unencumbered, totally freed of all mechanical, antiromantic contrivances.

I'm always coerced into going to weddings around here in Hollywood and I've done a little research about presents and their appropriateness, so here's the official word: The *smallest* piece of silver which can qualify as a wedding gift is a marmalade spoon of pusillanimous pewter.

If you guys and dolls are absolutely at your wit's end, and you feel you want to give a gift that keeps on giving, I recommend that you give a pregnant cat.

Now for an exciting romp through generalized circumstance, tossing off hints like rose petals in loveland. No problems now, for these tips will propel you into the winner's circle of discreet behavior and social adaptability. Here's how to become socially secure.

First of all, never pick your teeth in public, unless of course it's up off the floor. And when at a restaurant, be sure to

If you feel you want to give a gift that keeps on giving, I recommend that you give a pregnant cat.

whistle for the waiter with the correct fingers, those being the thumb and index of your moderately clean right hand. Furthermore, scratching yourself shamelessly, like an aging iguana, is uncouth, unless you turn your back on your date. If he or she becomes quizzical, just tell them in an offhand fashion that crabs are in season, just flown in from the University of Maine where you graduated Magna Cum Lobster.

For you girls who want to remain chic beyond repair, remember this: Ladies walking along the street after dark do not speak to strange gentlemen, unless they have been previously introduced or unless they, the ladies, are out of work with winter coming on.

For those afternoon garden parties, I want to assure you that it is now perfectly all right to sop up gravy with tiny pieces of bread, but not rushing from table to table. Also, when you walk, always carry yourself as if you're going to meet your lover, and if you must leave a calling card, be sure that the cards are clean, because just your name on the calling card is usually enough for identification purposes, without the addition of your big, juicy thumbprint.

It is bad manners for both men and women to blow on soup. Instead, it is regarded as elegant and permissible to pick up a napkin and swish it back and forth over the soup bowl, being careful not to let the ends dip in.

Remember that you can always carry a good thing too far, like politeness. I once knew a girl who was so pathetically polite that she wouldn't open a *clam* without first knocking on its little shell. And girls, it is now considered OK for you to powder your startled, gravy-stained face while dining in a restaurant. After all, no ladylike girl wants to shine in public.

A well-mannered girl will always step on her cigarette so it won't burn the carpet, and young ladies are reminded that it is not considered good form at formal afternoon garden parties to straddle chairs backwards and bellow bawdy barracks-room ballads. Also, if you girls are out on a date, don't wolf your food too hungrily; a really shrewd girl makes a man feel as if she's taking dinner *with* a man, not *from* him.

It is now considered cute, by the way, for a girl to have a toothpick in her mouth, provided it is protruding perkily at a jaunty angle. But never use both ends of that toothpick. And ladies, if you're tall and thin, and you insist on dancing with some guy who is short and chubby, remember that together you'll look like a beetle and a praying mantis and that's no fun at all.

For you dudes out there, be sure to tell your girl to hold still while you embrace her. Tell her not to move as one arm steals around her tiny wasp-waist, while another steals around her neck, and so on, depending on how many arms you have. If a guy tries to manhandle one of my dollbabies, I tell her to be sure to inform him that she has the mumps and they're incubating rapidly and will settle in his collywobbles.

Men, never try to blow your nose with a pipe in your mouth, and if you drink a lot, remember that it is now regarded as bad form in hypertactility circles actually to *lean* against a woman while talking to her. And when you kiss a lady's hand, avoid getting it wet above the second knuckle.

Ladies, if you're having a party this weekend, print this on a little card and stick it up beside the front door: "The Hardest Thing for Most People to Say in 25 Words or Less Is Goodbye." By the way, if your little get-together is just a tea, it is all right to hold out your little finger while drinking tea, but not with the teabag dangling from it, no matter how daintily you hold it up.

Now I shall point out a couple of embarrassing situations, and how to cope with them, hoping that you will be able to apply my advice to most of the detrimental social confrontations you might experience.

An ultra-chic girl, for example, is a doll whose cool is never shaken by anything; like when she spills cheap red wine in her lap, she doesn't care which leg it runs down. Easy does it with her, for beneath that layer of surface antagonism, there's another layer of genuine hostility.

The social disaster though, is falling down on a dance floor. Let me give you some meticulous guidelines to get you out of this predicament: Number one, you could just lie there; people will think you've had a coronary. Number two, you could get up with your date gracefully, and act as if your collapse were planned, as if you were demonstrating a new version of the Funky Pluck (which was invented by a hen while she was trying to hatch a hot potato). Finally, you could start mopping the floor vigorously with your handkerchief, and onlookers will think you work there. These insights will carry you through most terrifying situations. If, however, your predicament is unique, just give me a call, and I'll detoxify your head and sift through the shattered shards of your composure.

There's no better mask for a treacherous heart than an open, honest face.

Chapter Five
Bachelorhood

Bachelorettes

A bachelor girl is a girl who is still looking for a bachelor man.

A burst of Bill Ballance etiquette now—the ultimate in graciousness—manners, after all, are manners, even if they are vestigial. What I would like to deal with here is the type of woman who doesn't try desperately to restructure her female fantasies because she's already living them. She doesn't slouch around the house, full of gentle melancholy over a lost love, her soul stopped dead, drained of all vitality. She is a bachelorette, a seething mass of feminine wiles, standing there, erect and confident, grasping a large bouquet of glistening red, loose-lipped roses.

The bachelorette is the kind of girl who prefers to be a visitor in men's lives rather than a steady occupant. She prefers a confirmed bachelor because he's a challenge she can really pit herself against. Of course, there are all kinds of single, unattached girls, some of whom are single and unattached because of Mother Nature rather than their own preference. About as close one girl I know will ever get to being a swinger is through her erratic mental capacity: She has a mind like a bachelor's bed—never made up.

Some girls just don't have the right image. One doll who wandered briefly through my life felt a strange attraction for frazzled fur stoles that looked like something trapped in a drainpipe. She was a strain socially anyway, since her main private occupation was shampooing the tiny head of her inarticulate parakeet.

Incidentally, I'm not talking about that barracuda in boots whom we all know. You know the type—a lady of negotiable virtue who survives on her talent for intrigue and likes to drive everybody crazy, especially men, and then charge them for the ride. In her queasy quest for captivation—wearing her foxy feather boa, she spays every male within a two-mile radius.

No old or fat babes, either. You can always tell an unfrocked swinger by several long gray hairs spiraling off the top of her nose. These waspish old ladies, all hip-sprung and critter-bit, are going through a change of crinoline. And they always have orange or blue hair, and a swatch of crepe gathered under their chins in memory of their lost youth.

Fat women just never make it—their cheeks round and white, like a pair of suet dumplings. I'm sure you've seen these lardos, these gluttonous victims of self-inflicted calories, fat and soft, like a tomato that's been left too long on the vine. These porkers always end up at Adipose City, a retirement home for the gelatinous unwanted.

Other girls carry things to extreme, like growing blue-coraled teeth that protrude further out than their bustline. They go flinching through life, setting new standards for repulsion. One girl I fleetingly winced at was so homely that if she appeared in public she'd be arrested for disorderly conduct. Forget these human culls; they aren't worth the agony of public scrutiny.

Some little swingerettes carry the image consideration too far, feeling that they must look ultra chic at all times, and they wind up wearing a seersucker smock with matching tote bag full of Quaker Puffed Totes, or they've squeezed their component parts into an organically grown body-stocking with color-coordinated thongs. They think that *cool* is the only legitimate emotional response, that freedom from all authority is an unqualified good, that mobility as a life-style is far better than any sort of permanence.

Also, you men would be better off avoiding the little bachelorette who has had five husbands; that's five marriages down in flames, making her a nuptial ace. You're better off with the kind of girl who walks home from a car ride because she doesn't like the make.

Find a girl who doesn't think of men very often, but when she thinks, she thinks of men. I once was acquainted with a girl like that, who owned a comfortable place in the Hollywood hills, although when I knew her it did need a little air in the tires.

The nifty in question would undulate into a restaurant, and the waiter would always recommend frogs' legs served on tiptoe. Her physical presence was garnished with hash-brown eyes and moist, succulent, plum-colored lips. She was twenty years my junior, but one glorious evening I awarded her my official Credibility Cluster for closing the gap. Eventually, she married a politician and won the Watergate Good Citizenship Award. Now she's divorced and is senior charlady at the Hyperion Activated Sludge Plant, that land of fragrance and enchantment.

The way to tell a true swingerette, though, is with your eyes. If, for example, she likes to make the ski-bunny scene in her breakaway skin-tight, felt-lined leotard through which you can admire her beautiful triangular slalom, you've not only got a winner, you can count on her to stimulate your circulation both socially and venously. There really isn't anything like an adorable snow-encrusted face and supple bod, confined firmly in a pair of infra-red stretch pants with a secret compartment for her closed-ratio gearbox, schussing down the beginners' slope and into the mahogany splints of your emergency orthopedic van where you can teach her bones to knit.

Look for the bachelorette who is all outgoing and friendly, as if she's just emerged from a group-encounter session. Utilize caution, however, especially if she comes at you frantically emancipated, with something like this: "I have taken the pill, I have hoisted my skirt to my thighs, and I have dropped them to my granny ankles. I have rebelled at the university, skied at Aspen, lived with four men, and I have married twice. I have earned my keep, learned my craft, kept my identity, and frankly, pal, I'm lost." She now yearns to be over-protected to the point of harassment.

People with no kids have
only each other to spy upon.

Bachelors

A bachelor is an eligible mass of obstinacy surrounded by suspicion. He doesn't want a wife to share his life because most of those shareholders become directors.

The key to understanding a bachelor like myself is usually a three-part experience: First of all, there is the type of person he is, and the manner in which he projects himself; second, there is the place in which he lives; and third, there is the kind of car in which he tools around town. These are the most valuable ways of gaining insight into a bachelor's true private life (except, of course, by checking out all those sensuously voluptuous, exquisitely beautiful women he theoretically dates).

Some bachelors are . . . well, unusual, like a guy I once met who had two pairs of strings tied to his hat; one set ran down his sleeves to his wrists, and the other ran down his legs to his ankles, so that every time he tipped his hat, he automatically shinnied up a telephone pole.

Not all bachelors dramatize themselves that much, but you can always tell whether he's the party type if he likes to sit around with a lamp shade on his head, and with his cupped hands full of day-old confetti, prostrated with infatuation.

Many a contemporary bachelor was married as a teenager; he got bored looking for a job, so he plunged impetuously into the maelstrom of marriage—it was the only thing he could find that didn't require experience. Also, most bachelors have hobbies such as expensive cars and boats.

A friend of mine used to have a yacht—*The Tomcatamaran*— out at the marina, but then a jealous rejected girl friend opened his seacock, and it gurgled to the bottom. Poor devil. But I'd warned him not to turn her loose. She was complaisant and cuddly and wasn't leaning on him for that double-harness caper.

Another guy I knew loved to restore cars; he restored them to their rightful owners, after he'd gone joy riding in them. He made a handsome living as spraygun operator for a hot-car garage.

Automobiles play an important part in a bachelor's life. I remember one dude who had a car that had power brakes, power steering, power seats, power windows, and every other power option. He didn't even drive his car—he just sat in it and felt powerful. His secret ambition was to father a child by a girl from every country in the world.

You can tell when a bachelor really loves his car: When he scrubs out the tire treads with a toothbrush. A guy who used to do that drove a thundering souped-up Silver Cloud Rolls Royce with genuine Chippendale dashboard from which dangled a sluttish Kewpie doll. He called his car the "Spirit of Malibu," and he hurtled up and down the coast with incredible velocity, hauling his aspirations from one rendezvous to another. He's still a bachelor, old and lonely, because he didn't strike while his line was hot; he failed to embrace his opportunities.

Another bachelor I knew called himself an "automotive engineer"—he used to engineer girls into his car with only one motive. One time he had a phone installed in his Edsel, but all he got was calls from Packards.

You can always tell whether or not a bachelor is cutting a

wide swath socially if his trench coat is flecked with blades of grass. Sometimes his complicated life is like a Shakespearean subplot because of his blistering ego and his mendacious method of maintaining machismo. But the most dangerous part of all, and I now submit a gentle admonition, is that instead of being your fairy prince, evolved from a frog, he never becomes more than just your live-in horny toad.

No bachelor is a hero to his valet, not because the man is no hero, but because the valet is a valet.

Anytime I, a roving bachelor with a free-lance heart, get lonesome, tell you what I do: I crawl into bed in my bachelor flat and read about community property laws. Then I recite a penetrating rhymlet: Bachelorhood is just the knack, of loving without a heart attack.

Remember that what the well-dressed bachelor will wear while making love is his level head with its emotional gyroscope so he doesn't get too excited and suffer from premature jubilation.

I once knew an incautious bachelor who tried to make out with a meter maid, and was charged with "taking the law into his own hands."

A bachelor is a man to whom "two-o'clock feeding" is related only to nightclubs. He'd rather shuffle photographs than furniture. He wants those hands in his pockets to be his own. He'd rather cook his own goose. He has never met a girl he couldn't live without; he's a man of single mind and double-talk. He's a professional escape artist, and the only way a bachelor makes a good husband, is jealous.

A bachelor's favorite fantasy is that he invented sex, and that everybody practicing it owes him royalties.

A true bachelor is crazy to get married—and knows it. He gets tangled up with a lot of women to avoid getting tied up with one. When he's courting a woman he doesn't really want to marry, he murmurs, "Honey, tell you what—you set the day and the month, and *I'll* set the year."

A bachelor is a guy whose take-home pay doesn't *have* to get there. And speaking of home, a bachelor has a special kind of

A bachelor's favorite fantasy is that he invented sex, and that everybody practicing it owes him royalties.

comfortable, unshaven squalor to his life-style. Lots of women think bachelors are sloppy housekeepers who never make beds or wash dishes, and I want you to know that this is true.

There are certain secret little ways to thrive as a bachelor. For instance, I never let trash and rubbish accumulate in my apartment for more than just a few months. I simply keep kicking it around until it gradually disappears. I admit that my bachelor sty is a mess, and my dog keeps urging me to get married so his meals will improve. As it is now, he snarls every time I reach for the can opener.

I once considered lining up a live-in lovely who would also be willing to do my laundry and clean up the ankle-deep debris in my apartment. Of course I don't have any real problems getting my laundry done; it's only when I'm in a hurry that I dry my socks in the toaster. But you should see my kitchen, glazed with ground-in grime, and especially the sink, with its towering pagoda of dirty dishes.

In order to fit in harmoniously with the delicately poised ecology of my apartment, I've made friends with the mice and the bugs. In fact, I've trained a quarter-pound cockroach to bring in the morning paper. You've heard of places having a lived-in look; well mine looks wallowed in.

From the outside, you'd recognize my apartment by the olive drab lawn from which sprinkler heads protrude like iron dandelions. It's headquarters for National Rat Control, and is called "Chateau Rodent Refuge." But one of the charms of living in an elderly apartment building is the regular surprise syndrome. One morning, for example, when I shambled into my bathroom and turned on the faucet, it gave a deep sigh, then a deprecating cough, then finally ejected a small, indignant centipede into the basin. It was last seen scuttling after my cockroach and I expect the result to get a centerfold in the Entomological Digest. You'll never find any carnivorous insects in my apartment, though, because they all choked to death on the dust. Allow me to make an exception to that; I do remember one hapless cockroach that skidded and slipped to an early death on my

It's only when I'm in a hurry that I dry my socks in the toaster.

greasy stove. If I have any surplus food, I save it in the refrigerator until it decays. Then I make penicillin out of it.

I love to mutter and putter when I'm by myself. I shuffle around my apartment and, knuckling my forelock obsequiously, pretend to be my own aged, faithful retainer. I bow at my own brusque orders and murmur, "Yes, master." Actually, I'm much better off than quite a few guys I know, one of whom lives under an abandoned railway trestle leased reluctantly to him by Amtrak, despite the fact that he once held the Casey Jones Chair of Golden Spike Philosophy at Pullman University.

Another guy I know, a divorced type who misses his wife, gives himself sadly away every night, when the lengthening shadows under his eyes reveal that it's time for him to throw fresh sawdust on the floor, slip into his polyester coveralls, and coil up alone in his pint-sized pad at Shriveled Vista, a rural slum dwelling that's his shame and joy.

Nothing is more dismal than one of those so-called swinging singles apartment complexes. They are all stucco ghettos in which you are the stuccee. These places are merely dorms full of losers who get lonelier and dumber talking to each other in their one-room-and-percolator flats. Face it, a swinging singles apartment is mostly full of directionless dullards demolishing demi-johns of rum in the recreation area, and a few women over thirty, working off nervous fat in the women's exercise room that's always redolent of disintegrating dress shields.

One bachelor I know has a house on the lee side of an arid chasm. It's cantilevered over a steep drop, a perfect image of his high-risk career as foreman of a poppy plantation. In contrast to that, an extravagant pal of mine lives on a lavish country estate, so I call him His Rural Highness, and he says he's a bachelor because he wants to be a general practitioner instead of a specialist. Another guy lives so far back in the woods that for breakfast every morning he has owl eggs.

The most important part of any bachelor pad, of course, is his bedroom. A bachelor's bedroom is his private life, so if you pry open bureau drawers, like prowling through people's medicine cabinets, it means you'll probably come up with unwanted revelations. Petty vices are tucked out of sight, like a soiled handkerchief. Under a pile of linen you might come upon an intimate grief he's been trying to forget. It is therefore wise for you nosy dollbabies to respect his privacy as you occupy his bedroom and nestle into his receptive heart.

Some bachelors' dispositions oscillate between subdued rage and suppressed joy. Generally, though, we are a loving, resourceful lot, and we are convinced that nobody knows how to handle a married woman like a bachelor. This one morning, for example, I found a hole in my bodyshirt, just before an important date. Well, I didn't have a needle and thread, of course, so I stuck a flesh-colored band-aid over the rip, and then I pulled on my birchbark jumpsuit and took my girl canoeing as she strummed her catarrh.

A bachelor is adept at avoiding any and all forms of matrimony. He spends his time sampling baroque promiscuities, and enjoys home-cooked meals without marrying the dish. He admits with a smile that a bachelor is a selfish, calloused, undeserving man who has cheated some worthy woman out of an expensive divorce.

The best arguments for being a bachelor are the ones he doesn't get at home. A bachelor is a man who thinks before he acts and then doesn't act. He'd rather have a woman on his mind than on his back. His towels are marked "His" and "Whose."

Discretion is what a bachelor finally acquires after he gets too old to enjoy ignoring it. You can tell if he's a bachelor if he sits there and makes tea in a steam iron, but you know for sure he's married if he wakes up disappointed in the morning after dreaming of freedom. He assures himself that a wife is a great comfort during all those troubles a bachelor never has.

What a daily kick it is to be a roving bachelor. I live a hearty if somewhat primitive social life, and thrive on the wicked zest of being unfettered and unencumbered. Ah, the incessant rapture of total emotional freedom; I can go any place I want to and pursue any girl at any time I feel like it, which isn't as often as you probably think. And I'll tell you why I'm never lonely and don't miss either of my ex-wives: I have a fabulous water-bed that snores, gurgles, and grunts. Then in the mornings it waddles out to the kitchen and makes coffee. I'm now teaching it to nag.

Some bachelors aren't really the most convivial people around, though; I've listened to women tell me about eccentric dudes who will arrive for a date at the beach in a supercharged swept-wing Pierce-Arrow equipped with new carbide lamps, fresh tar paper on the running boards, a thatched fan belt, and flowers in its cloisonné vases. The guy will be wearing pistachio swim trunks, fitted with a secret flask full of enriched sage honey to revive his waning energy. And the only jolt he gets is jamming his beach umbrella into the hot sand.

Face it, chums, there are a lot of fringies out there. You know—guys who use an upraised hood of their car as an air brake, after being stopped by the police for screening porno movies on the wall of a traffic tunnel . . . the kind of guys who get Sears catalogues mixed up with copies of *Playboy*, and go crazy filling out coupons.

The typical bachelor is a guy who doesn't have to leave a party when he's having a good time. He's just a normal prag-matic type who realizes that a man can live much more cheaply without a wife. When a guy like this goes back to his hometown to visit his old haunts he usually finds that most of them have married. But he knows instinctively that moving from bachelor-hood to marriage means moving from the boundless to the bounded, so he maintains his tenuous freedom.

When a man is young, his mother tells him what time he has to be home and, when he's grown up and married, his baby-sitter tells him. So if he likes to roam totally untethered, he stays single.

Many of us bachelors finally learn to pace ourselves and not make love to the point of exhaustion. It pays to sort of hold back and not overrespond; after all, any axe gets dull if it's chopped down too many trees.

My own love life is as mixed up as a dog's breakfast, here, in Hollywood, where there are thousands of attractive girls in habit-forming quantities. And the only trouble with being a bachelor is that every once in a while homemaking rears its chintzy little head. My flat here at Jolly Squalor is so dusty that when the bread popped out of the toaster this morning it took me ten minutes to find it. When I open my windows, more dust, blows out than in, and I eat at different restaurants every night (I often invite girls up to my apartment just to see my collection of menus), and my coffee is so bad that one girl told me to hold the coffee and just give her the cream and sugar.

But I'm my own man. I come and go as I choose, at the behest of my free-lance heart, and I am unencumbered with the incredibly boring and trivial essentials of domesticity; I wouldn't have it any other way. The only thing that is true, lasting, and stimulating in all its aspects is independence. So here I stand, 5-10 in my socks, holes and all, readily admitting that in my apartment the only thing that is hung up neatly is the telephone. Why should I give up my hunting license when there .are still deer in the forest? Let me insert Ballance's Solo Law right here: To remain a woman's ideal, a man must die a bachelor.

> *Our lives are controlled by timorous*
> *old women dressed as judges; that*
> *obscenity ruling by the Supreme*
> *Court will make the world safe*
> *for hypocrisy.*

Chapter Six
Ballance's Handy Chops

This section will help others avoid disputatious dogs. If you happen to know that some girl is an authentic woofer, and you're asked about her, it pays to respond with a concise reply, not an outraged excoriation; I have found that the more devastating answers are always the most easily recalled, especially if you lay them on in authentic Rotarian Baroque. Consider the favor you might be doing someone who doesn't really know what he's up against.

I will now share with you some of my most astringent observations, all of which can be used with incredible ease. Tear this chapter out of the book so you can apply my Ballance Handy Chops any time they're deserved; carry these pages in your grubby pocket. Remember that economy and timing are critically important here, so that the person asking you for your impressions of someone else will come away with a clear picture only if you operate with smiling vituperation and say such things as, "When she cleaned the wax out of her ears, her head collapsed."

I remember being asked about a girl I once dated. Being a

rather diminutive doll, I merely replied, "She's so tiny, they give her electric shock therapy with a kid's joy buzzer." This not only gave my friend a picture of the girl's size, but also forewarned him about her state of mental hygiene, which he instantly asked about. "Her personality is split so many ways, her analyst has to use mob psychology on her," I smiled ruefully, adding that "her shrink got her a two-page spread in the *National Freudian Yearbook;* in fact, she was foldout flip in *Who's Who Among the Delightfully Deranged.* Her attention span is ten seconds, and seven of those seconds had better be a compliment. He then asked me if her looks were worth the psychological hangups, and I said, "Well, I'll put it this way— she's so homely that her analyst makes her lie face down on his couch."

All of this didn't really deter him, though, because he had his own problems, such as suicidal tendencies, which weren't helped much when his psychiatrist made him pay in advance. Later, he became famous in his neighborhood for successfully doing himself in with a slingshot. Poor devil had a complexion like an exploded anchovy pizza, and a father who was a certified Peeping Tom.

Appearances are important, so if a pal asks one of you guys about a girl who is an aggressive, surly hog, just say something like, "She has all the charm of a phosphorous grenade," or, "She has the personality of an untipped waitress." If that doesn't do it, say that, "She has a winning smile, but a losing face," or, "She should wear something simple to coordinate with her mind."

If you girls feel compelled to explain your reactions to a doltish date, just tell it head on. When asked, say something coy for openers, like, "Well, he's not exactly the embodiment of virility; he suffers from reverse charisma, if you know what I mean." When asked about his personality, say something like this: "His mind is like the land on his farm—barren by nature and impoverished by cultivation."

Sometimes people just don't get the word. If your girl friend persists in asking about another guy while she's out with you, say, "I think he ought to jack up his private life and change the tires, before someone kicks the chivalry out of him." That ought to befuddle her thoroughly, after which you might add, "Let me put it this way, he's a mouse with ambitions to become a rat"; or, "I think I'll go out and have a tree uprooted in his name—he has all the virtues I dislike and none of the vices I admire."

A guy is at a definite disadvantage when outlined like that, but it works two ways; sometimes it would surprise the same girl to hear him describe her as "an artful, triple-threat temptress who leases from Hertz Rent-a-Stud, and is now recovering from major surgery—she had her bosom recapped."

I found all of this very interesting, because she had described him like this: "He has a kind heart, but I refuse to say what kind; it probably comes from his origins, which are humble to the point of bleakness. Ever watch him make an entrance? The instant he strides into a room, he makes his micropresence unfelt." Both of these descriptions gave me clues about both people, but I made up my own mind about the girl after I learned that she got her start in show business as a singing flower girl at one of Lana Turner's early weddings. Her vocal coach said she'd have the most thrilling voice he's ever heard if her upper register had the power and clarity so desperately lacking in the lower. He said she certainly had an ear for music—too bad she didn't have the *throat* for it.

As for the guy, I decided he was a loser when he told me he loved uncooked bacon for breakfast, and he was always ready to lend a helping fist. I think he was German, because he was always sitting around scratching his umlauts. Personally I think he would be better off practicing full-time anonymity, because he got two-timed so much by his wives that he was awarded a PhD in cuckoldry.

One of his dates was arrested for felonious breast-feeding in public; this was in No People, Nebraska, a town that was so small they didn't have a village idiot, so they all took turns. He finally left in disgust and went into Midwestern radio. When I asked him how he was getting along, he told me: "Well, it's like being a mushroom. They keep you in the dark, they throw manure all over you, then you get canned."

This girl of his was a trifle top-heavy; in fact, her bras were manufactured by the Lockheed Helicopter Sling Corporation. But of course we all know that such beautiful curves are easily submerged under layers of flab, a terrifying development I will explore nauseously in another chapter. Even worse than porkers, though, are irascible women. At least you can see the fat on the lardos, but what do you do with a woman who is described as having "so many neuroses, she plans to issue them in a paperback edition?" That kind of woman never forgets a slight or remembers a compliment and usually has a vicious disposition, like a woman who got fat on bad food. A crow like that once beat me savagely with her crinoline parasol.

Then there are the girls who go through life being described as having "that respectful unobtrusiveness of one whose mission in life is to be totally ignored; the type of girl who would have been Phi Beta Kappa, but they ran out of keys." These women can really be exasperating, especially when they open their alarming mouths. Their tongues look like old avocado peels someone has wiped his feet on. And if you tell them they have mouths like gopher holes, they whine, "Your lip would curl too, if you had only one tooth to gnash."

Fast talkers can really drive you bonkers; one crone I know talks so fast that she says things she hasn't even thought of yet. A girl whose name I pronounce with panting reverence (she was a Tri-Delt known as Matilda Mastoid) had hash-brown eyes and a soft-boiled contralto, and that lovely voice was never quiet. I knew her at the University of Illinois where she was Coach of Colloquialisms. She finally lost her tenure and was picked up for disorderly desecration of the idiom. She was an odd mixture of the perspicacious, the perverse, and the preposterous, with a philosophy that goes like this: "If you can't say something good about a person, say it anyway, because somebody is bound to enjoy it." Or, "What you don't know won't hurt you, but it does give your friends a lot of laughs."

She had a roommate who thought that "charisma" was a

Mexican swear word. She was also a chatterer; in fact, trying to slip a word into any dialogue with her was like trying to climb on an elevator after it's started. She suffered from an unhealed wound—her atrocious mouth with hideous lips, thick, wet, and crimson.

Better to have a woman who is a credit to her gynecologist, even if she does wear so much lipstick that when she smiles she smears it in her sideburns. I knew a young, scrawny coed like that. Her arms were like buggy whips with fingers, but she was an inventive little thing; since she didn't want to hurt her digestion, she always plopped a Tum into her martini instead of an olive.

After a few high-voltage drinks like that, a woman can wind up looking like a freeze-dried nun, even if she does have a black belt in amorous macramé—the sinister art of stringing a man along.

I was once faintly attracted to the upper slopes of a bosomy young lady who insisted that her complaisant attitude was due to having been put asunder at an early age; this bombastically busty babe wore dresses so tight I could hardly breathe. She showed off every curve that was womanly possible. I loved it when she'd shrug her architecture at me. Eight years elapsed before I saw her again and she had changed a lot since I first met her; if it hadn't been for her ancient dress, I never would have recognized her. She used to have a great figure, but gravity caught up with her. She was so flat by this time that she was working topless at the House of Pancakes.

Her mother was a dessicated dowager who used to insist that she was bowlegged because of her extremely heavy pantyhose, but there was nothing wrong with her that a skilled taxidermist couldn't have fixed. And she had a topflight Neanderthal mind, too.

Sometimes I think I really prefer women who have seen more love than the rearview mirror of a taxicab. This is better than dating excessively grotesque girls who are so knock-kneed that when they dance too fast, they braid their legs. I recall a skinny girl whose head was always bouncing up and down when she walked so that she looked like an anteater picking out the fat ones. One time I overheard her say to another woman, "Let's not be catty, dear, although you *do* have the whiskers for it."

Some women have lips that look as if they're always talking through a megaphone, or they have a huge lower lip which passes unnoticed because it's covered by an even larger and juicier upper lip.

You can toss these off in your banter as you see fit: "She's said to be extremely rude to her inferiors—but I wonder where she finds them." "Is it true that Quasimodo was your posture teacher?" "You have enough dandruff to bread a veal cutlet." "I don't know whether that hair-do makes you look twice as pretty or half as homely." "I'm admiring that ingrown hair so neatly coiled beneath your skin." "If round shoulders ever come back, you'll be a superstar." "The shrieking of mutilated victims is the music of her life."

I once heard a woman described as having "a tongue so sharp she keeps snapping off the hem of her veil." This was possibly due to the fact that she also didn't have any chin, but you couldn't tell because her lower lip sagged over it. Frankly, this babe had her face lifted so many times she had to reach up over her head to blow her nose. She had a withered face like a bad almond. In fact, the nicest thing I can say about her is that she had a heart of gold with teeth to match.

The woman who tries to get away with being one of those "perfect combinations of imperfection" is a real drag, and usually has a nose like a hotdog bun; if she happens to have a million-dollar figure, her face is the withholding tax. And her legs are so bony that every time she sits down, her knees make a fist.

Women like that get jobs in the front windows of beauty salons, with a sign under them that says: "Ladies, don't let this happen to you!"

Having a sign around your neck is one way to fit a description, but I admire most the woman who doesn't demand alimony from her husband; she is grateful when he gives her outstanding references. Personally, I don't like snobs, or women with hair that looks like a cluster of uncooked lentils, so a well-recommended ex-wife with cuddling credentials is a good deal for an anxious suitor. Never look a gift horse in the proverbial, I always say—to my infinite ennui. But all of you must know by now that she absolutely must not be fat. There are tell-tale signs to warn you when you're gaining weight. You are more than just superpudgy, my dear, when your appendectomy scar is nine inches wide. As for facial features, of course we debonair types no longer say that a woman has a sagging double chin; a more suave description is "the contours of her face have softened."

Fat women, and particularly fat women who deny the obvious facts, are totally out. I always want to blurt something like this after I hear a plaintive fat denial by a female Sumo wrestler: "Oh no, you're not fat, you're just waterlogged, right?" Or, "Are those your thighs, or did your pantyhose explode?" Or, "You merely have an acute case of recurring baby fat, am I correct?" Or, "You just happen to have an ultra thick heavy skin, due to chronically enlarged pores, of which you have an incredible abundance." Or, "Chubby? You look like a honeydew melon with legs."

It irritates the living kapok out of me to hear denials of those hideous gelatinous facts. You know what I mean—statements like, "I just have a low center of gravity"; and, "I plan to lose several pounds tonight, playing my 80-pound banjo."

In a burst of physiological insight I one day deduced that women like this get their looks from their mothers, their intelligence from their fathers, and their figures from their stevedore uncles who steal heavy-duty brassbound girdles. These women usually have terrible figures, but sometimes they are able to hide them with bad posture. I said to one such girl who insisted on wearing micro-minis, "Such duds are not for you intended, unless you are diminuended." Poor burgeoning babe—if she had a little *more* where it *isn't,* and a little *less* where it *is,* she wouldn't have to tuck it in so much where it's *out.*

Now I don't want you girls to think that women make up all of the dogs in this world; only half of them. So if you want to brief a neighbor or friend or a two-legged canine of your acquaintance, a guy who is a picture of towering shoddiness (all windup and no delivery), with a phony smile that congeals on his sunken face, here are some tips of depiction:

You might simply come directly to the point and say, "His flawless character is marred only by his existence"; or, "He got that lump on his nose from nibbling cheese out of a mouse-trap"; or, "His outstanding characteristic is unrequited greed"; or, "I gag at the very mention of his diminished name."

On the other hand, you might indicate that he is a high-compression dullard, by saying, "He's like an old-fashioned kerosene lamp; you keep turning him down, but he won't go out." You might also indicate his age in a subtle fashion by saying, "His eyes are bloodshot today because of his teeth—he was up late last night looking for them."

Regarding his appearance, you can point out some little detail by saying, "I don't know whether that's a tie-tack or he had tapioca for lunch." Or you speak to him directly. You stare into his unprepossessing face and say, "I want to congratulate you on looking remarkably lifelike." Or, "Your visit has cli-maxed an already dull day." Or, you might say, "I don't know where he got that hair transplant, but his dog won't go outdoors without a bathrobe." Or, "Let's go someplace and commem-orate your lethargy."

If this loser is a real conversational zero, say something like, "He tries desperately to be hip, his conversation is full of oblique references to third world rage, neighborhood control, and confrontation tactics, and this loathsome gnome does all right until his personality starts to filter through."

If you are struggling for something nice to say about this guy, say something like, "Well, at least he's not contagious—probably because his germs are too weak to go on location." Or you might inconsequentially add, "And if it weren't for his scar tissue, he wouldn't have any character at all."

Perhaps, regarding questions of assertiveness, you might add, "I don't know how chicken he is, but right now he's home in bed with Newcastle disease." If quizzed about his independence

I don't know where he got that hair transplant, but his dog won't go outdoors without a bathrobe.

from Mom, just say that "he sounds as if he graduated with horrible mention from the Julliard School of Matriarchy."

Sometimes another woman likes to know about a man's stability, and if you are acquainted with him and have your doubts, merely point out that "he lost his mind once, but of course any such small object could be easily misplaced." "Still," you observe, "a man with his IQ should have a low voice, too." And if she wants to know how to whittle him up, she asks him, "Is that your face or did someone clean a fish?" or, "If Moses saw you, there'd be another commandment"; or, "Here comes an ugly rumor looking for a place to begin"; or, "You are the perfect refutation of that theory that everyone is put here on earth for some special purpose"; or, "Every man has his price, but you hold bargain sales"; or, "You'd make a great staging area for a typhoid epidemic"; or, "He may be colorless but he's certainly not odorless"; or, "He has the type of personality that makes instant enemies at friendship clubs."

If you find yourself searching for something intellectually redeeming, just say, "He does have a good head on his shoulders . . . but I think it might look better on his neck"; or, "When small talk is sufficiently minuscule, he can nearly hold up his end of it"; or, "In cerebral matters, he's working himself up to nonentity." Finally, just sigh and reluctantly murmur, "I'm afraid he's getting by with rather slender mental equipment"; or, "I've never heard of him, but of course I never read the bankruptcy notices"; or, "Poor guy—he used to be known as the boy wonder . . . now people just wonder . . . as he goes through life arousing vague, unallocated repugnance."

> *I never believed there was*
> *life on other planets till I*
> *saw you troweling pancake*
> *makeup over your third eye.*

Conversational Counterpunching

Introductions are always the most difficult part of any conversation, particularly if you are only semi-alert and you are accustomed to having other people introduce you to all of your social contacts. In times of stress, when you find yourself overcome with convivial urges at festive functions and you are lacking the necessary assurance to circle in firmly for the kill, merely fall back on my special lapel-grabbers, offered forthwith.

The only requirements, once you summon the courage to activate one of my forensic fuses, are probity, wit, understanding, and verbal dexterity. It also helps if the person to whom you have unceremoniously attached yourself has not been recently lobotomized. Remember, chums, looks can be deceiving. But now I'll help you achieve your primary objective—getting your splayfoot in the door.

Frontal parryings are the main social responsibilities of men, hence most of these opening moves are so phrased. You girls pay close attention, though, because some of you are forthright and aggressive hussies, and I love you for it. If you find a line that you can toss a lip-lock over, you have my permission to pluck it out of these pages like an aphid off a rose bush.

You dudes attending a party or possibly a private screening of the latest erotic extravaganza, suppose you see a lovely, winsome thing idly gazing off into space, her eyes shimmering with rudimentary intelligence, all alone and begging for your special brand of attention; you suavely sashay over and murmur, "Hi—you are rapidly melting my permafrost heart here on the frozen vastness of this troubled planet." Try not to hesitate or stumble, and avoid being singsong.

Once you have her attention, you quickly add (before she focuses her unaligned molecules), "You look as if you are suffering from badly shriveled self-esteem—may I be of some assistance in restoring same?" The gallant gentleman gambit is usually more than somewhat effective, but if you've annoyed her, and she replies acidulously, "No thank you, I don't want to complicate my life, especially with someone who walks as if the load levelers in his high-rise jockey shorts are askew," it's wise to fade over the horizon, popping your gum nonchalantly so she'll be impressed at your sang-froid and colossal cool.

If your ego is as frail as a moth's wing, and you feel compelled to insert the last word, zap her with, "You are a girl of angelic restraint, exuding an air of synthetic benevolence and neo-goodwill, so I'll cut the conversation short, lest we both fall prey to verbal overkill. Anyway, you've given me a brief, chilling hint of your relentless self-preoccupation, so ta-ta."

The best lines must sound spontaneous and unplanned, to avoid the above-mentioned conflicts. Thus, it's wise to begin with either a compliment, like, "I was just admiring the wonderfulness of your escalating bosom and had to meet you"; or an offer, like, "Let us take tea together and exchange sympathies, my dear. One never knows what might happen, does one?" Then you go click-click with your favorite eyelid, and make sure it doesn't stick shut.

Sometimes a reference to her intellectual prowess can turn a girl on, like, "To me, you appear to be a lady of surpassing insight—are you introspective, my dear?" If she has a little moxie, she replies, "Why yes, of course." You instantly rejoin with a flourish. "You have just defoliated both lobes of my brain plus my heart and adjacent giblets." If you think that's too overwhelming, say, "You have just subdivided my heart into quivering gobbets of cardiac tissue." By then you should be securely rooted in the vestibule of her psyche and in the hem of her skivvies.

If, however, your potential plum does not appear to be a Renaissance woman, but her bodice is firm and full, just open with something like, "My Queenly captivator, you are revealing definite outcroppings of sheer magnaminity, and besides that, I enjoy beautiful women because it rests my eyes."

We are sometimes confronted with people whom we have once met and would rather forget, so when they're introduced to you for a second time, the best line is, "I don't recall your name, but your nullifying breath is familiar." Or, if you met her once before, and you want to make a favorable impression, say, "Yes, we've met briefly, and during that interlude you administered extreme unction to my composure"; or, "I've heard a great deal about you—of course it was all *whispered*"; or, "Hello there . . . tell me, who wears your *clean* pantyhose?"

If you are introduced to an appalling dog, the best thing to do is to be casual and elegant, but disassociate yourself by purring, "My dear, you've curled up my heart like a salted snail, and I'd like to hug you closely, but I might crumble these graham crackers in my shirt pocket. So, despite our memorably brief encounter, I am filled with an enormous sense of loss and loneliness at our having to part. Call me sometime right after the first of the . . . century."

There is always the chance, however slim, that you might pick a saucy, sassy winner. If so, give her a preview of things to come, by saying, "My darling, alone at last—one false move and I'm yours. Extend your swanlike neck so I can implant thereon a mammoth cerise kissing-hickey."

But if she comes on chilly, keep your cool, and mutter, "Dearest lady, I never forget a confrontation with an attractive woman, but in your case, I'll make an exception." If she doesn't shave fastidiously, be sure to point it out gently by saying, "My love, you might well profit by a little deforestation under your arms."

If, however, she is the delicate type, say something like this: "Let me gaze into your disconcerting eyes, and, if you wish, you may sob ecstatically on my shoulder and mildew my costly jacket." This approach is probably the most sensitive, and therefore one of the most effective. At this juncture, however, your problems have only just begun.

> *He is not only dull himself,*
> *but—even worse—he is the*
> *cause of dullness in others.*

Light Sparring

After introductions, the step which follows usually emphasizes some light sparring in the parry-and-thrust division of human relationships. Since this chapter is devoted to Ballance Handy Chops guaranteed to clear the air, we will assume that things have not really worked out to their best advantage. In other words, you find yourself dealing with the ballast of humanity while trying to sail the carefree seas of conversation. Proceed on this premise, and open with a remark like: "Well, to me you sound as if you're going through a change of linen"; or, "Without your makeup on, you look like an old leather book that's been chewed on by a puppy"; or, "You're a nice girl, but you have scum on your ankles."

After an especially dull exchange, you might smile: "You've just attacked me with a blunt instrument—your wit." If the tableau has been exclusively one-directional, and fatuous, you grin reassuringly and say, "I must admit that you are a virtual storehouse of gentle misinformation, and I am grateful to have been inundated by your excruciating banalities."

After a rambling journey across Tepid Terrace you add, "I would like to compliment you on your keen sense of the lugubrious"; or, possibly, "There seems to be a paucity of communication—that wasn't the most illuminating dialogue of the day that just cascaded from those cracked lips." But if it was especially tedious, say, "Give me a few fleeting moments to grope my way back to reality after that massive blast at my serenity"; or, "You may not have shown much sparkle in that exchange, but you certainly were avidly inept. But don't be discouraged—there's *got* to be a future for you; after all, they made penicillin out of moldy bread."

To those chilling, emotional barrages, the best thing to do is calmly reply to your antagonist, "Do I detect repressed hysteria in your tremulous tones?" That really drives them up the genuine lath-and-plaster wall, after which you can bring them down with, "Your logic is as convoluted as a conch-shell, but you win the Nobel Prize for cloying and coy connivance." If, however, you are trying to draw her out, say something like, "Let's explore the delicate spires and turrets of those medieval castles you build by cantering across the demure drawbridge of your heart."

Sometimes that works too well, whereupon you ejaculate, "Well, now that we've come to terms with mediocrity, let me assure you that the greatest remaining undeveloped territory is between your ears." If you've got a real gabbling blabber-babe on your hands, say, "What a talker you are—I hope you haven't dislocated your tongue; I haven't even had a chance to wet my lip!" Finally, if she is constantly making grammatical blunders, interject, "Well, I always say, if you're going to speak just one language, speak it *good!*" Or, "I hope your intentions are better than your English." Or, "You must be on a nastiness high."

After a particularly shrill encounter with a human reed-squeak, demand a replay, asking in your best soft-boiled bari-tone, "Tell us, in your most violent contralto exactly what happened, so we can continue this effortless flow of polished inanities." If she complies, and ends on a devastating crescendo, just murmur reassuringly, "Well, that's how the herring mari-nates, but I did enjoy the fading splendor of your shopworn little voice."

People with bizarre speech patterns deserve special attention, and when they are a drag, they should be told so. Something like, "Your voice is husky to that fascinating point just short of asthma." Or, "You sound like a hyena with boils." Or, "Is this the voice that launched a thousand Nodules?" "Listen, weasel-head, the stridency of your drillmaster voice is matched only by your cesspool personality." If it is an emotional encounter—"Your voice is quivering like an exposed nerve—it sounds as if you've just hauled yourself out of a melancholy reverie by your bootlicks."

It also pays to let people know you're well aware of their vocal calisthenics. Comments like, "Your heretofore gentle, well-modulated voice is growing a trifle abrasive." Or, "You sound all penitent and remorseful—or is your esophagus back-firing?'' Or, "You sound massively frustrated—are you suffering from laryngeal polyps which are probably not benign?'' Or, "You don't sound very friendly; why don't you chip a little of that ice from your frosty tones?'' Or, "Your speech is little more than a festival of grunts. I'll bet you graduated from elocution school Phi Beta Glottis.'' Or, "As a trained observer of human behavior, I'd like to suggest that you knit yourself a new head.''

A happy greeting is always well-received, especially if it points out something as personal as an individual's voice: "It's so good to hear your friendly shriek, your well-modulated bellow again,'' will always please. In fact, if someone says you have delusions of grammar and then gives you a heartfelt "Boooo,'' you retort, "Same to you, lover, only half a tone higher.''

If you are trying to deal with a standard-chant type who has a cumbersome way of expressing himself, mutter in your cor-rugated bass, "You have an interesting way of speaking, as if you select each word with a pair of tweezers.'' Or, if you wish to simply terminate your suffering, just politely say, "You are rapidly worming your way out of my confidence so, please, from now on, don't menace me with your friendship.'' Or perhaps, "You suffer from halitosis of the intellect,'' or, "The only thing you do beyond the call of duty is to make sure you can't *hear* it.''

Being direct always has its advantages. People like to know right where you stand, especially when you urge someone to "skip the facts and get down to the slanderous whispers.'' It is even more endearing when you are constantly correcting them with zingers like, "I think you have a flawed sense of reality,'' and, "Cliches flourish in your speech like crabgrass on your lawn.'' The best thing to say is, "Let's not *mince* words—this isn't *pie* time,'' or, "With that Southern accent, you sound like a hound dog lapping clabber out of a jug.''

There is nothing quite like squaring away some malcontent who is having personality problems. They thrive on hearing someone say, "You seem to be suffering from a running feud with yourself," or, "Your personality is likely to disintegrate under its own inbuilt stresses, so why not accelerate your crack-up?" After receiving their thanks, reassure them by saying, "That's sort of a left-handed compliment, a distinction equivalent to praising a cow for depositing the roundest pie in the pasture."

If your opponent takes false pride in his mental attainments, whittle him down to size with dignity: "I did not say you're *wrong*—I merely pointed out that your work has yet to be fully tested and evaluated by the scientific community; it seems to have some of the vaporous quality of your delusions and suggests a logically consistent theoretical edifice built on scientifically untenable premises. In another cerebral dimension, your reasoning remains relatively sound, but your judgment and ability to test reality are seriously impaired because the only thing you can keep in your head over an hour is a cold."

Conversationally, there are few things more insufferable than a nonstop talker, a monster of garrulity. Have no mercy—cut him short with: "Your speech is a major contribution to the delinquency of both logic and syntax, but luckily that endless bobbin of words within you seems to be rapidly unreeling." Follow this up with: "Why don't you go down the corridor and take a hiatus?" After the word-mangler is through, say, "Thank you for having stockpiled so many bromides." And to those who are a geyser of vocal inanity, it's always effective to inquire: "Do you ever have an *unexpressed* thought?"

People who love to talk about their amorous gamesmanship are among the dullest. They never learn that today's loving entertainment is tomorrow's amorous artifact; they've failed to absorb Ballance's How-to-Stay-in-Laryngeal-Harmony-with-the-Universe Law—that the crunch of communication is *now,* that we speak with our lips to *explain,* and with our throats to *convince.*

If people think they have been wronged, they deluge you with bruised emotions, in voices drenched in disenchantment. Tell them, "I notice that your capacity for self-righteous anger has scarcely been tapped, and that, offhand, you have a definite flair for self-annihilation." Finish them off with, "You seem to be deeply ensnared in a cluster of romantic sub-plots, but ironically enough, you are always ready to defend your most precious possession—abysmal ignorance," or, "If they ever tax brains, you'll get a terrific refund."

The traditional bore can be dealt with in the same manner, especially when you say, in curmudgeonly tones, "Our dialogue has become as wooden as a baseball bat factory"; or, "Your logic is foaming on the rocks of accuracy." The indirect compliment sometimes is effective, provided your meaning is clear: "The grandeur of your gabbling makes me want to explore that mind so full of skimpy knowledge." Follow with this: "You have chilled the marrow of my head with your fluent Icelandic." Or, "You have lots of character—and it's all weak."

People who think they live in sparkling fiscal elegance tend to give you swollen pecuniary glands; to prevent this, just rasp: "From the dollar signs in your voice, I'd say you've been sipping a little tincture of avarice. And even though you do have a certain dash, your dots are missing." Continue the dissonant dialogue with a semicompliment: "Thank you for your alertness, whenever that was—I really admire your magnificent contempt for common sense." A wise old philosopher, either I or Mark Twain, once said: "Give a rope of patient silence to a boring intruder, and one day you will hear that he has hanged himself." To those suffering from fiscal flatulence, you can always chop: "I wish you were an asset so I could liquidate you." Or, "You have all the compassion of a vivisectionist."

If someone in a group is boasting about his dynamism, you might galvanize them with: "Have I told you lately that you are noticeably nondescript and that I worship the ground that's coming to you?" or, "I didn't say you're a bastard, I merely observed that your paternity was, and still is, swathed in the mists of time."

Taken altogether, light sparring is an accumulation of quasi-pleasant attention-grabbing zappers which help to put adversaries into proper perspective when they suffer from verbal dropsy. Tiny endearments like, "Yes, my blemish?" work wonders, and comments like, "You are a master of the precisely inappropriate word," or, "My dear, compared with your ideas of logic, palm-reading is an exact science," can really obliterate mealy-mouthed meanderers. But from here on there is really only one way to go if you are trying to prevent someone from launching into a long-winded, self-caressing monologue; let us head now for our next pusillanimous plateau, because we are long overdue for heavy blows, thundering denunciations. No longer will we speak guardedly, like convicts in a chow line.

> *"Why, you regressive turgidical,*
> *pigeon-breasted, pencil-necked,*
> *acne-maculated lounge lizard."*

Heavy Blows— Thundering Denunciations

Heavy blows are churlish chum chasteners, authentic toxic put-downs. They are meant to be used sparingly, as most of them are devastating indeed. Be forewarned; most people would prefer not having a heavy blow dealt them, even if their conversation is little more than syncopated emphysema. These are high-voltage zingers for those with eczema of the psyche. Don't try to elude them; just stand back and assert yourself, saying something none too soothing, like: "You have the personality of a temporary filling." Or, "Thanks for the inspirational sentiment; it should be engraved on the head of a friend. If silence is golden, you'll never be accused of hoarding."

Perhaps you find yourself confronted with an obnoxious woman lecturer who feels compelled to tell you all about her countless platform accomplishments. You say: "The most eloquent lines are not spoken, they are worn." Or, "I notice that as the evening wears on, your face wears off." If she has an edgy voice, and she isn't particularly witty, say, "Your voice may not be mellifluous, my dear sacrificial heifer, but it certainly is caustic," followed by, "Sounds like you just arrived at your wits' end, after an incredibly brief journey." Or, "You are preserved in the aspic of your own self-esteem." As you leave, say, "You may not have been the most articulate person I talked to today, but you have had me listening with nothing less than feigned interest." Or, "You should be preached to death by wild, hormone-injected curates."

Now here's how to distract and silence irritating people at a party: Sit at their feet and silently mouth every word they say, making sure the individuals actually see your elaborate lip movements. This never fails, and it's an exclusive Ballance production I developed while studying Pidgin Berlitz.

Sometimes a person who thinks he's especially intellectual can be extremely aggravating, and intensely deserving of an introduction like: "May I present the once and future Has Been?" or, "Your face is familiar, but that's all I can say about it." The most crushing blow to a pseudo-intellectual would be: "You've just given me wonderful revelations; you've brought home to me so many things that weren't familiar to me before . . . but of course my dog does the same thing"; or, "Is it true they're training a white rat to replace you?"

If her stomach rumbles and gurgles, don't rudely ignore it; swivel your wise eyes her way and smirk: "Undergoing a little seismic disturbance in your lower strata?" Then dig her in the ribs and chortle, "Well, you're only human."

If the dialogue was tinged with a hint of superficial sadness, you might say, "That was heart-wrenching; it makes me want to fling myself in front of an onrushing glacier." Perhaps another direct, frontal assault could follow, like, "You don't sound very friendly or happy; your quartzlike voice is colder than an unheated cathedral. Your chilly tone is like a breeze off the freezing tundra."

Maybe you're just minding your own business and somebody

insists on relating their intimate love problems. If it's a woman, say, "Your guy doesn't sound oppressively intellectual or intimidatingly bright, but you know, from his mother, he derived his love of books, and from his father, he derived that sick and oppressive love he has for his mother"; or, "He never struck a woman but once . . . and even then, it was unfavorably"; or, "You know why he talks so much—he's wearing his wife's teeth."

For an extremely oppressive personality, you might say something like, "My dear, you're a credit to your race—the 4th at Santa Anita." Follow that with, "You seem to have an uncanny talent for making and keeping instant enemies." If she dares reply, say, "Well, we've just reached a nadir of nitwittedness, but there's nothing wrong with you that reincarnation wouldn't help." Or, "Your complexion is a perfect example of the risks involved in deferred maintenance."

For those aging dowagers, point out that "you were never lovelier, my dear, and I think it's a shame." If she persists, agree with her, to a certain extent: "Yes, your beauty is evanescent—in fact, I can still see traces of it."

When confronted with a dreary drab, tell her that you admire her "tireless pursuit of mediocrity." If she persists, say, "You're not very pretty, but you make up for it by being totally devoid of talent and charm."

If it's something like personal appearance that's hurting your mind, say something like this: "Is that your nose, or a wart that made good?" Or, "I'd like to congratulate you on your successful battle against personal hygiene," followed by, "You have brains, all right, but they're not mates." Terminate the situation with, "Remember now—if I should ever refer to your beauty, I'm only reminiscing." Or, "That's the most attractive tufted mole I've ever seen."

Girls, if an ingrate is hassling you, and you feel his attentions are a little too intense, you might say to him, "You have a mouth that should be kept in the woods to trap varmints"; or, "I notice that gravity has been tugging gently at your jowls." If he is a real oaf, tell him, "Why don't you come over to our

Hawaiian luau some time, and don't forget to cram an apple between your teeth"; or, "Have you been crying? Your face is clean"; or, "He's suffering from a severe bone deficiency—there's not enough of it up and down his back."

Sometimes people who are just plain dumb are the most deserving of a handy heavy blow. Say something like, "Listen, fishlips, the nicest thing about being stupid is that you don't have to fake it, right?" Or, "If you had a brain operation, it would be minor surgery." Follow all this with, "Your importance in my life can never be underestimated, probably because your mind has lost none of its vacuity and you are totally free from the slavery of awareness." You might add: "When brains were passed out, you were busy demanding a second helping of mouth."

A wonderful greeting can also square away a slob, especially if it's delivered enthusiastically, like, "Good morning! What can I do for you—and remember, I'm not a plastic surgeon." Another effective greeting: "Hi—what a great looking outfit. Tell me, who makes your stains?" Or, "Is that your real complexion, or did your body paint spread?" Or, "You look like someone I'd avoid at the laundromat." Or, "Congratulations—you have just established a new frontier in tedium." Or, "You represent the marvelous consistency of the uninspired."

If you're out on a blind date and the situation has turned irrevocably sour, turn to her and ask, "Didn't you share a bone with my dog the other day?" Or, "Have you been running? You smell tired. One more warm day and you'll spoil." Or, "When the human race went to the post, you must have been scratched." Or, "Your character is mediocrity compounded quarterly."

There are all kinds of ways to make your feelings about someone clear, like, "The last time I saw a face like yours it was plunging into a feedbag," or, "The last time I saw a mouth like yours, there was a hook in it," or, "Your sense of dedication is matched by your absence of talent." More specific approaches include lines like this: "I'll drive you around town, if I can find a harness to fit you," and "Girls like you don't grow on trees—they swing from them." Or, "I'd like to find out just what it is about you that endears you to no one."

First impressions can trigger final responses, like, "Please, I'm getting indigestion just from your breath," and, "Would you be interested in telling me your *dull* life story?" Or, "I couldn't warm up to you if we were cremated together." Another winner is, "You look lovely tonight, my dear, you must have gone to a tremendous amount of trouble"; or, "Is that your face, or did somebody empty a bedpan?" or, "How good to see you again— failure hasn't changed you a bit"; or, "Didn't you have the leading role in *The Romance of Rubella?*"

If you immediately decide that a person will never even meet a modicum of human decorum, say, "I guess I'll have to learn to live without your love—as so many of your friends have." Or, "Someday the worm will turn, and when it does, don't forget to put your hand out." Or, "You never looked better in your life—whenever that was." Or, "I gag at the very mention of your diminished name." Or, "You exude a certain elfin charm which I find absolutely resistible." Or, "With just a little more warmth, you could become a morgue attendant."

Little things can offer insights, so point out certain attributes that you think might have a lasting impression, like, "I just noticed your hands; how are things at the lube rack?" Another insight might go like this: "Are those new earrings, or are you just a sloppy eater?" and, "Your teeth have become stately, moss-covered ruins." Or, "Who does your nails—the gardener?" or, "If you had your teeth in, I'd make you eat those words"; or, "Your layer of cordiality veneers a tough thickness of total opacity."

So heavy blows are those you do not wield unwarily. It pays to check out the size and weight of your target, lest your features go through a sudden reorganization. If you're attacked, shrug it off by reassuring him of your amiability. Say, "I admire you—your blundering is so versatile and your face is unclouded by thought"; or, "Hmmm, steam heat seems to bring out your natural bouquet."

It pays to check out the size and weight of your target, lest your features go through a sudden reorganization.

The progression, however, now approaches its final phase, which, of course, is the Last Word.

> *"Well, I see that your infatuation*
> *for yourself has burst into flame*
> *again."*

The Last Word or Ultimate Epithet

The last word is uttered when there is nothing left to say, or no point in saying anymore. To have the supreme advantage, it is best to be in transit, and be sure to turn your back on your opponent's tiny, bite-sized head. Pause briefly, turn and blurt: "My dear, the only things we have in common are irreconcilable differences"; or, "You smell as if you have been rather skimpily embalmed." "Have you finally learned that Beaudelaire is not a refrigerator?" "There you are, demonstrating your limitless incapacity."

Another, more vindictive approach is to depart laughing, saying, to some sluggard whose pep-pills have flamed out, "Why don't you put your false teeth in upside down and chew off the top of your head?" Or, "Sweetheart, I forget your name, but I remember your facial." Or, "You're like the bottom half of a double-boiler—you let off a lot of steam, but you don't know what's cooking"; or, "They say that beauty is only skin deep, and it's women like *you* who keep saying it"; or, "You have long since worn out your ne'er-do-welcome."

For those of you who are more subtly inclined, you might simply take your leave while saying, "Isn't it wonderful how the body carries on after the brain is dead?" Or, "Your misfortune fills my glands with gloating"; or, "You're so homely, your wife gets combat pay"; or, "I treasure every minute we're apart."

When pushed to excess, you might quietly leave and softly sniff: "Someday you're going to go too far, and when you do, I hope you stay there." Or, "You have about as much heart as a stalk of nightclub celery."

If your adversary is a shambling derelict, addicted to clown-sauce, don't be too harsh; merely remark, "I'm not implying that you drink a lot, but is it true that you consider the corkscrew the world's finest precision instrument?"

The light-hearted approach is usually much more satisfying, because you rarely have to purge yourself of bitter guilt recriminations. What you say is something like, "Why don't you go down to the local animal shelter and give yourself up?" Or, "You are nothing but a loose thread in the tapestry of life." Or, "You're a belch with legs." Or, "Have you been gargling with cauliflower juice?"

The best thing to do, though, is to simply clear the air, without malice, and say, "If it weren't for her goiter, she wouldn't have any figure at all." Or, "You are rich in reprehensibility." Or, "Why don't you go join your ever-widening circle of enemies?" Or, "Your inscrutable smile stretches across a chasm of incompetence." Or, "He looks like everyone's son-in-law: intensely sincere and stunningly good at nothing." Or, "Why don't we make you a cardinal so we don't have to kiss anything but your ring?"

> *"If that's your
> exit-line, why don't you
> follow it out?"*

Chapter Seven
Family and Relatives *or*
Nothing Propinks
Like Propinquity

If you feel like an emotional basket case due to the strain and pains of those around you, namely your family, relatives (all of whom are inherited critics), plus that Super-Mom from Double-Motherland, just stay with me, a Cum Laude Manipulator from Tumescent Tech.

Don't race off to a summer resort—that's where nobody knows how unimportant you are at home—and don't dismiss everything so airily. Join GMAC (Great Machismo Aids Communication), stand your turbulent turf, and hang in there with me. I will provide the necessary insights and phraseology; you provide the action.

Let's start at the beginning: babies. Babies are a nice way to start people, but if a couple's first baby ever knew how little information his parents had about him, he'd demand to be kept in the hospital those first few aching months. I was so small and weak when I was born, my parents were going to drown me, but they were too embarrassed to be seen carrying me down to the river. They would have been bitterly sorry because two years later I was cast as the original constipated Castoria baby.

Some children are born independent and self-reliant—like me, for instance. When I'd wake up squalling and wet and furious, I'd get up and walk the floor by myself—actually, toddle. Why, I used to clamber out of my aromatic crib at dawn, crawl out onto the service porch, then wash and iron my own diapers . . . for which my grateful nurse would croon, "Thanks a pantload."

The only help I ever had when I was first born was when my nubile nanny was kind enough to wash me. Unfortunately, she also hung me on the line to dry, which is why my ears are shaped like they are. I was born at exactly 5 a.m., and I remember it clearly, because I had to reach over and shut off the alarm. I was such a homely baby, my Dad refused to put my pictures in the family album—he'd only stick in the negatives. He was so ashamed of me that at least once a week he'd leave me in my baby carriage parked in a tow-away zone. Believe me, I had just as tough a childhood as the next braggart.

Watch out for babies with voracious appetites, because I recall that at the age of eight months I was eating solids— crayons, bottles, newspapers, and sawdust from my Dr. Spock doll. They used to feed me through a funnel. Like all babies, I was nothing but an alimentary canal with a mouth at one end, and no responsibility at the other.

The most important thing about babies, though, is that they resemble their parents, even in their first, early infantile moves. My dad and I were a lot alike when I was a baby; my sister could tell the resemblance right away. For one thing, we'd both fall asleep over our bottles.

Children are the next step, and most of them can be rated like movies. A teenage girl is, for example, a young woman who looks G, acts GP, and daydreams X. It is wise from the outset to avoid comparing your kid's behavior with your own at his age. You may resemble each other, true enough, but things are totally different now from the way they were. Just remember Ballance's Evolutionary Law, in couplet form: "The grimmest words of pen or tongue—"We didn't do that when *we* were young."

We've all somehow survived that alarming disorder known as

Why, I used to clamber out of my aromatic crib at dawn, crawl out onto the service porch, then wash and iron my own diapers.

adolescence when we were full of fierce, exultant vitality. Some of us became disaffected rebels who considered chaos a prerequisite to salvation; some became dropouts, idle and derisive. Many of us grew long, shaggy hair, and every time our complexions cleared up, our minds got mottled. Of course, the hippies are gradually sinking back into their quagmire of despond. These misfits never realized that they were just as vulnerable to the follies, cruelties, and excesses of the hippie world as they were to those of the straight world they'd abandoned. And the real reason they didn't trust anyone over thirty was that they didn't understand them, and they were afraid to try.

Nature wisely gave us twelve years to develop a love for children before turning them into teenagers. But I was always a smartass, and I mean right from the start. One time at a family party in Peoria, an elderly aunt gave me a wet, hairy kiss and asked me what I wanted to be when I grew up, and I said, "An orphan." On opening day of first grade, the teacher asked, "Billy, do you know your alphabet?" I snarled, "How could I? I've only been here ten minutes." At long last I now realize I was an Apprentice Demon, and I finally understand why—every time I threatened to run away—my Dad begged me to put it in writing.

It was at this significant time that I formed my first definitive doctrine, one that has since come resonating down the corridors of time and distance as the Ballance Cardiovascular Law: "Emphatic denunciation of the young is a necessary part of the hygiene of old people, and greatly stimulates the circulation of their tired blood."

And now I must caution you—never spoil a child. There is nothing more atrociously cruel than an adored child, a supertot who is always writing such insidious pamphlets as *How to Phase Out Mom and Dad.* She demands that the world conform to her uncontrolled desires and emotions, and it's our own fault. Society has provided her with so many escape routes that she never has had to stand her ground against disappointment, postponement of pleasure, or the weight of responsibility; all of which are forces that shape character. Thus she continues through life, demanding that she get her way, and when she is frustrated, she pushes, antagonizes, challenges, and, finally, runs away—usually into the dismally destructive drug culture, a total flight from reality into a fantasy world, squandering her health and damaging her brain.

Some kids never really feel secure; one day, for example, I asked my Dad piteously, "Don't you want me?" He snarled, "Listen, pal, the only time I wanted you was before you were born." This kind of attitude can definitely warp your élan, and at an agonizingly tender age.

If you supply your kids' needs, believe me, they'll supply their own wants. For example, children never think it's fair to give them, as a gift, something they can wear. To the average child, a gift is something he can set adrift, or shoot, or ride, or throw, or shake, or scare his playmates with, or break. That rhymed and I heard it somewhere years ago, so if you're the author, don't come whining to me.

Little girls are the ones who really grow up fast. Many parents of a female teenager think she's nothing but a surly ingrate; they forget that her body is undergoing profound physiological changes, that her entire endocrine system is altering her emotional and mental functions. Before their startled eyes, she is metamorphosing from a baby caterpillar into a fluttering butterfly. Before you know it, the tiny dollbabies in frilly feminine frocks are women in blue jeans. Perpetual prepubesence can get stale, though, like the little girl I knew who had a full head of curls when she was small, and her mother wanted to clip them off, but her dad wouldn't allow it. He always used them to polish the car.

When I was a kid, I was so anemic that my teacher used me for chalk, and I remember when I had measles, the kid next door fed me sodapop with a straw shoved through our diseased letter slot. I was a tough and unruly boy—in fact, I was so irrepressible that I didn't go to a regular kindergarten. Instead, I was brutally consigned to the Federal Nursery for Delinquent Infants.

The first thing little children learn is which parent gives in the easiest; little girls quickly learn it's their dad, and they have him under control from then on. This practical kind of education is always more crucial than reading, even though books for little kids are much better these days. Remember that one about Jane, Dick, and Spot? Spot was a dog, and Jane was nothing to brag about.

Everybody knows that the only thing more annoying than a precocious child is her mother, because besides sugar and spice, little girls are also made of curiosity, cantankerousness, and pure, unalloyed guile. And what happens to little girls when they don't lick their plates clean? Well, for one thing, they grow up to be high-fashion models. Little girls want to be *princesses,* but little boys don't want to be *princes,* and from those two different starting points come all the confusions and cross-purposes of courtship and marriage.

Kids can be a great comfort in your old age—and they help you *reach* it faster, too. Some parents would like to unload their offspring, however, like a guy I know who has a couple of ultra-homely daughters; he's so anxious to get rid of them that he holds regular elopement drills.

You wonder how I knew that my Dad hated me? Well, he was constantly searching for loopholes in our relationship; in fact, one time I caught him trying to erase his name from my birth certificate. The poor devil sired me late in life so that by the time I came along it was too late for me to change his bizarre behavior patterns. He was always examining the seams of his life, looking for lint (represented by me) and his office was finished in nutty pine.

Sometimes I think I had it better with loving indifference than smothering attention. I never enjoy seeing parents springing at their children like an avenging shrike. Or the kid who's so accustomed to chiming in his two-cents worth that everytime his mother opens her mouth, her child pounces on her like a duck on a Junebug. Best thing to do is to send your kids to bed while you still have the strength or send them off to camp every summer.

Summer camp is where parents spend $500 for eight weeks so that their kids can learn how to make 25-cent paperweights. Summer camps are getting more progressive, though. No longer are kids taught leathercraft and ashtray ceramics; now they get a crash course in campus disruption, creative vandalism, non-bathing, the care and handling of Molotov cocktails, and bank bombing. At summer camp I was always called a "real beaver" by my counselor; not because I was eager, but because I was always saying "damn" while gnawing on a pencil.

Teenagers are a different category. Girls never mean the bitter things they say to boys, nor the sweet things they say to girls. And the easiest way to tell a 15-year-old girl from a 15-year-old boy is this: Her feet are bigger. And it's easy to see when your daughter is growing up: She dresses slower and dials faster. Acne (Puberty Enemy Number One) also has a tendency to set in, along with a bundle of teeny-bopping nervous energy, and the female kidlet regards a parent as the sum of the squares on both sides of her family.

Thus teenagers are usually balanced precariously at the end of their parents' patience, and the worst misfortune that can happen to an ordinary teenager is to have extraordinary parents. Ever watch the offspring of celebrities struggle to match their parents?

Sometimes I really believe that the only culture that teenagers are exposed to is bacteria. I knew one young girl, for example, whose parents wouldn't let her swim out in the ocean in the Santa Monica area, because they were afraid that she'd leave a ring around the pier. She's long since grown up and has become rich, thanks to her invention of the Midol popsicle.

What is home without a teenager? Well, it's a great place to rest, which is something a mother of four can barely remember. What we really need is a child labor law to keep teenagers from working their parents to death. It all works out though; a teenage girl who never pays any attention when she's called is the girl who grows up to be a waitress. The *ideal* parent is one who makes himself progressively unnecessary; teachers and parents exist to be grown *out* of.

Kids race through the kitchen like starved hurricanes, getting refuelled in midair and ready to cruise the drive-ins and impress each other in that ceaseless reconnaisance known as teenage, so always keep a chilled platter of wolverine fetlocks from the International House of Botulism on your coffee table.

Heredity causes a teenager to wind up with mom's eyes and dad's car, and revisionist history is what contributes to all the communicative cobwebbery between teenagers and parents. It is written as Ballance's Law of Adolescent Ennui that parents never know how much they *bore* their kids.

Personally speaking, I want you to know that I'll never forget my mother and father; why, they were almost like parents to me. Still, I know how to tell an involved parent, and particularly an involved mother. She's the one who hopes her daughter will find a better husband than she did, while knowing full well that her son will never get as good a wife as his father did. But of course fighting and screaming and yelling and brawling is good for kids. It prepares them for marriage.

Relatives, of course, are worse. Admitting a mistake to an in-law, for example, is like bleeding in front of a shark. Relatives are always meddlers; always nudging, always prying, always making insane demands on you just because, through a biological accident, they're related to you. Relatives are the revolting spies of life, and if just once we let them into our lives, it opens up new vistas of discord and mutual disapproval. To avoid tribal tribulations, always keep relatives at arm's length lest they get a greedy grip on you.

I have more relatives than a microbe, and without exception they all urged me not to continue on radio after I graduated from college. Well, I'm still on radio. It may kill me, but at least it's been feeding and often clothing me for a lifetime. Sticks and stones may break my bones but it's a living.

Nothing is more disturbing than families linked together by mutual dependence like an emotional chain-gang. One of my in-laws, for example, had a lot of phony pride in her family. She claimed that one of her royal ancestors suffered a fatal shoulder wound while being knighted by King Arthur. One girl I knew could actually trace her family tree all the way back to the days when her family lived in it.

By the way, my Grandma—who is now 98—was a pioneer groupie; she used to follow the John Philip Sousa Marching Band around the country; she had the scorchies for a certain snare drummer who named her Miss Rimshot of 1900.

I remember one of my mothers-in-law got sore at me for revealing on the air that one of her forebears was the only pilgrim to make a round trip on the Mayflower; he got turned back at Plymouth Rock as a security risk. She also got all sick and nervous when I announced at her family reunion that, after careful, painstaking, historical research I'd learned that she was right; one of her ancestors *did* march in the Crusades, but it turned out he was a spy; in fact—just like her—he was a double agent.

Here's the real problem with visiting in-laws: Their short-coming is their long staying.

In-laws are always nudgy, but I've figured something out after years of vigilant observation and reading Tolstoy: All happy families *resemble* one another, but every unhappy family is unhappy in its *own* fashion. And the only thing you get for nothing these days is relatives.

> *For every man who's teaching his son to be thrifty, there's a woman teaching her daughter to be extravagant.*

Mother-in-Law

This mottled, senile old crock deserves a special subcretinous category. The typical mother-in-law is a grim-faced malcontent, who sets out poisonous pannikins for harmless butterflies. She looks like Godzilla on her daintiest days, and most of the time her peaches-and-Gainesburger complexion dominates her rotten character. She gives off a sustained peevish whine, like the skirl of bagpipes.

A mother-in-law is more than simply a relative. She is a bustling, fluttery, noisy nuisance. I fondly recall naming one of mine "The Warthog." She was so harsh and cruel that one time while eating her heart out, she broke a tooth. She always wore some sort of lacy, beer-stained ruffles around her withered throat, where crepe had gathered in memory of her lost youth. Ballance's Olfactory Maxim: Mothers-in-law always smell their age.

One of my mothers-in-law was a handy crone with the sauce; she used to put a dab of Napoleon brandy behind each pendulous ear, then she'd try to make herself kissable by dipping the ends of her fierce white cavalry mustache into a beaker of liquified Binaca. This harridan, this vitriolic virago, was completely grey, except for her hair, which was orange. She drove a cab, and worked as a part-time bouncer, and when she arrived at our house for her annual infestation, we had to serve her meals in a special serrated receptacle to accommodate her beak.

She was always an indecisive old scold. She could never decide, for example, whether to go to the movies on the weekends, or take a bath. I can still see her, sitting at the head of the table, grasping her Field Marshal's baton. She's the one who got a stern warning from the board of health, and then, when she was finally forced to bathe, she got both feet stuck in the water pitcher.

Most mothers-in-law are fat and loud and coarse, but they repel me anyway. Somehow she manages to make the most of the faults she has. She tries to inflict her hangups on those who have blundered within earshot of her demands, and if she's crossed in any way she sets off in her defiant waddle, taking her daughter with her. They both then project a haughty silence, and stalk stiffly into the enveloping mists like puppets with snarled strings; they walk out of your life on stilts of scorn.

I can still see her, sitting at the head of the table, grasping her Field Marshal's baton.

Mothers-in-law are freelance emasculators who aren't *born,* they're accumulated. One old babe I knew with jumbo legs had to be lowered into bed with a derrick. At dawn, angrily-muttering retainers hoisted her out of that same bed with a windlass, forklift, or stump puller, depending on how much of a load she had taken on overnight. She was so grotesque, it took a Polaroid an hour to develop her picture. I used to call her "Lunar" because of her cratered face; about the nicest thing I could say about her was that she had a coated tongue.

Now don't misunderstand me; I was always generous with my mothers-in-law. One of them I gave a pair of sequin-studded culottes to wear while she was out digging postholes. If you're thinking about giving your gnarled mother-in-law a gift, I can recommend many appropriate presents, most of which I have given in dreaded years gone by.

An official Bill Ballance Missing Person Kit, with full instructions on how to become one, makes a splendid personalized gift. So does an aerosol can of feminine hygiene spray filled with corrosive Essence of Persimmon. I also recommend a fifth of high-octane thalidomide, laced with low-voltage muscatel, to make her life a trifle more palatable, and blessedly brief.

A 32-gallon plastic trash can—big enough to hold the old walrus herself—is always a big hit with her hostile family, as is a portable, zircon-encrusted bidet, with a secret compartment for cyanide pellets. A gold cigarette case, in which she can carry her teeth, comes in handy, as will a Polish parachute for those adventurous, skydiving grannies. A Polish parachute, of course, opens on impact.

I even got an ex-mother-in-law a job once, down at Camp Pendleton, teaching the Marines how to fight dirty. Now she lives out at Sedentary City, a retirement community for Unfrocked Hussies and the Senior Unwanted, known among geriatrics nurses as The Vegetable Bin. The best gift of all, though, and one by which she will always remember you, is a harelip decal, guaranteed to get her a million laughs at family reunions.

This last gift should contribute to your mother-in-law's insecurity, and it might even stimulate her hypochondria. One of my mothers-in-law even had a tachometer on her pacemaker. She was once voted Fishwife of the Year by the Common Scold Society of North America.

Another thing most mothers-in-law seem to share in common is a gluttonous appetite. One time at a barbeque, I watched transfixed as my mother-in-law wolfed down four pounds of food off a paper plate; she then licked the plate, then she burned the plate and inhaled its nutritious smoke. For dessert she shot up fermented curare and then picked at a bowl full of marinated rutabagas like an anxious raccoon.

Food intake like this, with sidedish platters of catfish smothered in crawdad sauce and pulverized live bait, have a tendency to make the muncher appear less than feminine, which she was. The pleats in her neck stood out like contour plowing; she was a great hulking porker, a Puritanical hardliner, a self-righteous prude whose varicose veins crawled like fat blue worms under her sensible rayon stockings. But at least she was self-sufficient—she used to cap her own teeth and detach her own retinas.

One of my mothers-in-law was a really tough, leathery old iguana; she enjoyed her coffee strong—in fact she ate it right out of the can with a spoon so that those little flavor buds could burst into life as they churned expectantly through her pyloric sphincter. She was the one who woke us up one morning rattling the bars of her cage because we'd forgotten to give her a basin of fresh water the night before. When company came, we kept her chained to an iron ring in the floor.

Another of my mothers-in-law was a snob, and always spoke in an accent that suggested an inadequate education at the Sorbonne. She loved to spend the entire weekend in her garden, weeding by mouth. She was a zealous environmental crusader, and loved to race out to the parking lot and sniff exhaust pipes so she could check the bio-degradable level of their exudation. She was the same crow who was called to Mt. Palomar for the dedication of their sundial and abacus; they wanted someone who was around when they were invented.

This ex-mother-in-law of mine looked as if she'd been carried out of Shangri La twice by the Dalai Lama. Just for chuckles, I used to stuff her pantyhose full of walnuts to make her jogging less comfortable. Why, she thought Jack the Ripper was a great social reformer.

A friend of mine got married so many times that he married one of his former wives twice without realizing it. He never would have found out except that he recognized his mother-in-law's snarl.

One of my mothers-in-law liked to caper around the house with the wind whistling through her threadbare knickers. All that leaping around caused her ankles to sag over her wedgies so she crammed the flab into corrective crinkle-boots. She had a head like a distant neutron star—a superdense concentration of matter. I can still see my sodden mother-in-law standing naked on our front lawn, shouting outraged obscenities at the neighbors, and lowering property values for blocks around.

Be extremely wary of your mother-in-law; listen carefully to her, sprawled out there on your warm patio, poisoning the minds of your kids against you, pouring cholesterol into the familial arteries, spreadeagled in the sun, with small, easily fooled children swarming over her like horseflies on a beached whale.

Most mothers-in-law wear chips on their shoulders like epaulets, and they love to brood in their vulture's nest. One of my mothers-in-law had the slender face of a pensive baboon; her cranium was long and narrow, suggesting intelligence, but actually she was more crafty than profound. She was the one with no teeth at all, so she had her gums enameled. With that tile rim on her upper and lower jaws, she had a grin like a vicious bathtub.

Have you ever noticed that when two prospective mothers-in-law convene, it's like a meeting between two horse-traders; each one of them is suspicious of what the other is unloading. That's because a mother-in-law is like a referee who has an interest in one of the fighters. And one admonition—don't overdo matrimony; a third marriage is like buying stock in a falling market.

I always suggest that you guys elope. That way, if you're lucky, her family will never forgive you. If you fail to offend your in-laws at the very onset of marriage, you're letting yourself in for years of relentless meddling.

> *The honeymoon is over*
> *when the quickie before*
> *dinner becomes a Martini.*

Chapter Eight
Women

In my affectionate study of the female universe, I have learned that never in the course of human history was so little known by so few about so many.

I think real women should have what they want and deserve, but those harsh, strident, unfulfilled womlibs have too many male hormones; those hairy faced, bandy-legged, metallic-voiced nonwomen spoil life for genuine, lovable, real women who don't want to be lowered to "equality."

Most male broadcasters prize women for the same reasons they prize a ribbon-winning Dalmatian—they seek a fineness of line, a glossiness of pelt, an aristocratic stance, and, above all else, an alertness to command.

My attitude toward women concerns my response to them, and not necessarily their response to me. I think it is important in any relationship not to ask for any more than you're willing to give. I love women; it's a habit I formed years ago instead of biting my nails. All my life I've enjoyed women, from their earliest infancy to that grim day when, full of withered malice, this tormented old trout is heartlessly consigned to that Dumping Ground for the Dying, that Warehouse for the Unwanted, a "retirement community," where tireless Time assaults her body, but her mind remains alert enough so that she realizes how much old age is like teenage—it's a time of waiting before that big trip into the unknown.

I've always enjoyed hugging and nuzzling and kissing women, and I've never been one of those "Ball-Bouncers" who likes nothing more than sitting around locker rooms, struggling to be a rugged back-slapping pal, thrilled by pungent sweat socks, and disintegrating elastic. They get their thrills being with other jocks. That's not for me. I hang around women—I enjoy their company and their beauty and their charm.

But listen, my problem with women is that I want them when I want them, not around me all the time. I need time to ponder, to meditate; I thrive on solitude and carefully-timed aloneness. All the women I've known say they "understand," and they murmur reassuringly, "I'll just sit in a corner and be quiet; I won't bother you—honest, I won't say a word, I'll just watch you work."

Not a single girl can seem to get into her tousled head that a woman's biggest mistake is to be there when a man doesn't want her; it's almost as bad as not being there when he does want her. The waters of logic may lap unfelt at her feet but who cares when you feel that certain trembling in your eager loins?

All of this enters my mind every time I'm confronted with one of the greatest and most stimulating sights known to man: You're stopped at a traffic light and a high-stepping strutter springs off the curb and prances across in front of you, shoulders back, stomach in, and with the kind of swivelling, tuck-under walk that let's you know that she is proud to be a healthy woman. It's a sight guaranteed to warm the porcelain cockles of your solonoid. And no guy likes to operate with cold cockles.

> *A woman is no sooner ours than*
> *we are no longer hers.*

A Woman's Outlook

A woman's outlook involves her emotional circuitry, her intuition, and her approach to the complex problems of everyday existence on an instinctive level. When a woman is not in love, she can be as cold-blooded as a criminal attorney, and yet unrequited love over the man who got away is a woman's natural nourishment, and she thrives on it.

Individual women differ alarmingly; one lovely critter likes to bite it out with enraged mongooses, while another wrestles alligators in a sideshow. But on the surface they are gentle fawns beneath whose exquisite carapace there beat hearts of pure marshmallow.

Sometimes personal problems arise from a woman's basic outlook on things, like secrets, for example. The way a woman keeps a secret is handy. It is an absolute fact that women can keep a secret every bit as well as men. However, it is also an implacable fact that it takes more of them to do it. Never tell a woman anything in confidence because a woman is born with a syndicated tongue; to her, a secret is either too good to keep or not good enough to keep, so she hushes it about from friend to friend. The length of time a woman can keep a secret depends on how quickly she can reach a phone; so I now implore you to remember Ballance Law of Revelations: A man never tells his wife a secret. He just thinks he does.

There are three ages of women: Girlhood, middle age, and "you're looking fine." And because women are hyper-sensitive, a thoughtful man will always be primed with gentle repartee. For example, at a party, if a woman accuses you of not remembering her, you retort heatedly, "Not *remember* you? Why, my dear lady, I've been trying to forget you so I could carry on my life."

All any woman really wants is security and a chance to play with insecurity. Otherwise life gets tedious—sitting around blanching almonds, whiling away the hours wondering whether she should join the hard core of the outer fringe. Of course there's nothing worse than those addled brides who race around the house, bursting with spurious vitality, all hot-eyed and uncomprehending, spinning their wheels. They're so anxious to please their new husbands that they wash the goldfish, then climb up on the roof and vacuum the inside of the chimney.

There are all kinds of extremes, though, like one baleful babe I know who exemplifies the waste and confusion that makes up the lives of most women without direction or purpose. For these women, the central emotions of their lives become boredom and apathy. Part of this problem stems from the fact that women often find themselves prized and yet ignored; prized as an object, yet ignored as a person. It is this situation which makes it tough for them to perceive the prison they occupy, so they attribute their unhappiness to faults and neuroses within themselves. Our woman is confined to a domestic dungeon. She is captured in a nylon noose; she's the victim of galloping, unplanned parenthood. After a few years, her marriage becomes an unrelieved and debilitating debacle; she's irrevocably hooked up to a dude who got married merely to qualify for wife-swapping parties.

Women live in a world of emotion; men rationalize. This polarizes them into separate worlds. A man, once committed to a woman, feels that this is the end of the story; a woman, committed, is certain that this is only the beginning. She never learns that the only things perfect mates come in are shoes and gloves. Hell, I know a married couple who despise each other, but it's working out great because all married people should have something in common. They don't separate because they are so used to each other's vile habits; they don't really want to bother to develop fresh patterns of rancor for any newcomers in their lives.

A man knows he's in trouble if, after having committed himself, he comes home to find his mate frugging around the kitchen, sipping a Purex martini, and fantasizing about weightless passion in a lunar module. She is a perpetual teeny-bopper, sitting around in her slip, her breath scented with licorice jujubes. She rushed into wedlock as a teenager, in defiance of all the warning signs. Better for her to be goal-directed and active, even though she's tottering through the day with real tots.

Women enjoy nurturing their fantasies, cherishing their romantic dreams, and staving off those recurrent daily dreads. Sometimes things can get a little piercing, though, when she sees herself as a failure, all negative and ugly-grubby, and she builds on her self-seen inadequacies and reaches a crescendo of self-pity. Going with a troubled girl like her is like riding on a condemned roller coaster; while you're hurtling along, banking on those upcoming emotional turns, you know something's wrong, but you cling on, and after it's all over, pal, you really know you've been someplace.

Watch out how you part from her; women understand being phased out, but they will never forgive being treated with contempt. Ballance's Departure Maxim—a woman will forgive anything but being treated disdainfully. She doesn't, however, mind doing that to you, and then asking for mercy, so always remind yourself that next to inflicting the wound itself, what women make best is the bandage.

There are basically two kinds of women in the world: Those who take a man's strength and those who give a man strength.

Women are dangerous domestic pets, always ready to slip their leash, and always in need of a distemper shot. And where money is concerned, they are like a dog with fleas; they can't rest as long as they have any.

There is nothing more disquieting to a hard-working husband than to come home to someone waiting in her wrinkled cotton housecoat, with two buttons missing, and loose threads dangling. This is the woman who still has a smudge of powdered sugar on her upper lip from eating donuts for breakfast, washed down by coffee so weak it had to be helped from the pot. She has long since learned that nothing stops a woman's tears quicker than a man who pays no attention.

Sometimes you find an inventive girl who has restlessly contrived homemade contact lenses out of Kaiser foil, and hopes somehow to kick the oatmeal habit before the onset of

Where money is concerned, they are like a dog with fleas; they can't rest as long as they have any.

middle age, as she gradually exchanges her emotions for symptoms with a proud haggard smile. She learns that middle-age is when the narrow waist and the broad mind change places.

There are many astute allegories involving women, but my favorites involve both cats and snakes. First of all, women and cats enjoy boredom and derive great strength from it, whereas men are exhausted by boredom. Secondly, women possess all the more likable characteristics of serpents. They share the same subtlety, the same propensity for getting around things, and, of course, both women and snakes capture a victim by fascinating him and thus rendering him helpless.

In public, a woman without a man looks forlorn, but a man without a woman looks romantic. A woman can radiate total charm and warmth and immediate empathy, but most of the time she relies on her intuition—which is nothing more than man's transparency—and winds up yanking the panic cord, letting her vitality be eroded away by anxiety and torment. End result: Domestic debacle, the clues being nervous titters from too much coffee, and an absent-minded running of her hand over her twitching face, as if to slowly wipe away that invisible web of regret and sorrow.

It is a dismal time; those melancholy sighs as she mopes around the house, waiting for something wonderful to happen in her drab life, full of daily trivialities. She strives to orchestrate her household chores, and finds herself abstractedly drying her hands on her mynah bird. If she's healthy, her face should be crinkling into jubilant puckers, unmistakable patterns of joy and delight at being alive and active during these Surly Seventies which will seem so picturesque a century from now.

A lot of women are like refrigerators; she slowly gathers an ice formation over the years, which, if allowed to accumulate unchecked, will reduce her operating effectiveness to zero, at which time she needs emergency defrosting, for she knows that the hardest meal for a housewife to get is dinner out. So here's how to hint—greet your man at the front door wearing a striped prisoner's suit.

A woman's most basic need is to be loved, while a man's

most profound need is to be admired. When she is well and truly loved, a woman never develops that peering snarl on her face, like having the sun in her eyes. She avoids self-pity, and the erratic approach to housework that culminates in bursts of rapidly waning energy and headlong exasperation. Every day she is subjected to the tyranny of domestic togetherness, immersed in a whirlpool of dull and transient household chores which are totally remorseless. She knows she'll never get caught up with them for keeping house is like endlessly stringing beads with no knot at the end. When she and her family go to bed at night, everything's done, but while they're sleeping, sheets are wrinkling, dust is settling and stomachs are getting empty. And then her husband makes her punch a time clock when she starts preparing his breakfast.

All any woman wants out of life is a passionate husband and a few other guys she can compare him to.

A sure sign of despair in a woman is when she wears too much makeup and not enough clothes. She is thigh-deep in shrieking toddlers, and is preoccupied with the past, daydreaming about what might have been. She has learned to her sorrow that husbands are like boys who have had the mischief taken out of them but the inclination left in.

A man is always surprised when he discovers that a woman is totally incapable of feeling love for an automobile or a motorcycle. She only pretends enthusiasm for his toys. She will willingly sacrifice her life for the man she truly loves, but this very same girl will break with him forever over a matter of pride. She will never forgive being treated with scornful superiority.

Women gain power over men by giving us intense pleasure; when a woman is a terrific lover, her man slowly comes under her domination. She has learned how to pull the lanyard on his psyche. For beneath the soft and sensuous surface of every woman lies the cool, calculating almost diabolical intelligence that is capable of using every desirable inch of that lovely exterior to direct, control, and otherwise captivate the helpless male. And sexuality lasts as long as life. People finally stop having sex the way they stop riding bicycles—because it looks ridiculous, because they're not spry enough, or because they no longer have a bicycle.

Woman, the eternal paradox, strives to make her man subservient to her will, while subconsciously hoping that her efforts will fail. She knows instinctively that the difference between a successful marriage and a mediocre one consists in leaving three or four things a day unsaid, that the success of any good marriage depends on the partners outslying each other.

I know these things; I've been down that road and can give directions. But after two marriages, it'll take an awful lot of butter to get me back in the frying pan. One of my wives used to get up in the morning, throw back the drapes and yell, "What a beautiful day to spend money in!" One time she growled, "I'd go home to mother if I had anything to wear." Nothing to wear—and eight closets to keep it in. Why, she had so many clothes jammed into her closets that the poor moths never had enough room to learn to fly. So it's no more marriage for me; profligate pursuits such as repeated matrimony soon exhaust a man's energies and disperse his wealth.

No one hates to hear a woman admit her age as much as her twin sister. Twins never can seem to forget that they're part of a litter; I used to go with an identical twin, but I could never trust her. Everything I'd tell her went in one ear and out her sister. I finally had to jettison her because no matter what we did or said, it was as if everything was being enacted in the presence of her twin.

Women are inclined to love men for their character, while men tend to love women for their appearance. And most women don't need to be actively happy at all—what they really need is a feeling of being *envied*. Friendship between two women is always a plot against each other; life is a hard, unceasing battle between a man and his enemies and between a woman and her friends. Have you ever noticed how all women treat one another with occupational suspicion? Friendship among women is only a brief suspension of hostilities, a fragile nonaggression pact soon to be broken. Jealousy is the friendship one woman has for another. But what a dismally drab world this would be if women were as homely as men. It is written as two separate but equal Ballance Edicts that the animal in men that women really want to bring out is the beast of burden and that the difference between a man's wife and his mistress is about twelve dollars a meal.

Ballance's Stipulation has it that you should *never* put a woman on a pedestal, for a woman is like a bird; look up to it and what happens?

A friend of mine was involved with one woman who had such a vicious temper that he had to shoot her regularly with a tranquilizer gun; the unfortunate critter had learned to hate in equal proportion to her inability to charm. A woman's influence is in exact proportion to her charm; and, of course, charm in a woman is what backbone is in a man. What all women want is a man who is strong but gentle, a benign dictator. It is inscribed as Ballance's Prismatic Law of Reflection that when a woman gazes into a mirror, she smiles, but when a man looks into a mirror, he frowns. She is practicing gentility and he is struggling to project fierce masculinity. And marriage gives them both a binocular view of life.

A woman's image of herself is often that of a spoiled child who tries to rule by tantrums, followed by sudden bouts of love. Every woman under thirty thinks she's an actress, and every actress thinks she's under thirty. A pal of mine is dating an actress and they're an ideal couple—hopelessly compatible; they both laugh at the same things—his wife and her husband.

There is not much to choose between a woman who deceives us for another, and a woman who deceives another for ourselves. But, chum, you know the honeymoon is over the first time she snarls, "You'll do nothing of the kind." An experienced married man is one who can tell when his wife comes to the end of one argument and is beginning another. The last word in any domestic argument is what a wife has; anything a man says after that is the beginning of a new argument.

If women really knew themselves, the fact that men do not know them would flatter them less and content them more.

Tears comprise the hydraulic force
through which masculine willpower
is defeated by feminine water power.

A Woman's Train of Thought

A woman's thinking process involves the most circuitous logic and the most roundabout method of doing things that is conceivably possible. There is no real method or order to this phenomenon; it just exists, chum, so the best thing to do is relax and enjoy it. Avoid puzzled hostility at all costs; it isn't worth it. Understand that a woman thinks the way she does because she's a woman. If you try to take it beyond that point, you have your head up and locked.

Some women like to work their problems out slowly, like a Scrabble player short of vowels. But you've got to remember that women are like money; keep them busy or they lose interest. A woman is happy when she gets the man she wants, not the problem solved. Men are the problem, and a woman is happier when she gets the man every other woman wants.

A woman's shopping list is a good example of controlled chaos. It is a masterpiece of obsessive compulsiveness, and usually leaves their eyes twinkling with inward cunning.

Virtue in women is often merely love of their reputation; intelligence is more like money—that is, if she doesn't reveal how *little* she knows, people will assume she knows a great deal.

Sometimes you can tell what's on a woman's mind just by observing her behavior. If, for example, a woman is wearing a miracle-crepe housecoat, and she lets it swing open seductively while she's waiting for the mailman to arrive at her front stoop (actually, her stoop is off scuffling for a buck), chances are that she isn't really expecting an air mail special, she just wants to be stamped "fragile."

Fifty percent of the world's population is female, but somehow women always are a novelty. A woman's train of thought contributes to this effect, especially when she thinks of ways to be helpful and save money, for example, by breaking off one prong on all the household cord plugs, so that, logically enough, the electricity bill will be cut by half.

Hell hath no fury like a woman hunting for a new lover. Young girls compete for dates, while middle-aged women hang on desperately to their mates, and lonely old widows huddle together for comfort. A female is faceless unless she sees herself reflected in a man's eyes, and the only way she can ever seriously reform that man is by boring him so completely that he loses all possible interest in life.

Most women have the same philosophy as the government; they never let being in debt keep them from spending. Also, when a woman says, "I won't mention any names," it usually isn't necessary. That's because women love to hear something and then spread it on the phone; they hear a choice tidbit and instantly wear out their dialing fingers.

Maybe it's a good thing men *don't* understand women; women understand women, and they don't like them. But women without horse sense become nags, the kind who have icy thoughts of vengeance as they pluck the morning lint off their braids while hunkered down at their vanity tables, muttering imprecations against the world.

At a social gathering, nothing can stop a talkative woman in the middle of a sentence like the arrival of another woman— with two men.

When a woman wants to be taken at her word, she means her last one, and all women are attracted to the strong and silent type man—they think he's listening.

Remember, girls, *how* you apply your lipstick is not nearly so important as on *whom,* and when one woman talks it's a monologue, but when two women talk, it's a catalogue. And as far as politeness among women is concerned, it's always an alert truce. Most women will agree that when a husband is overly anxious to please his wife, he is either being cheated on or intends to cheat. She may even admit that a husband is a man whose pursuit of happiness cost him his freedom of speech and that a married man is a prisoner who thinks he has the run of the jail.

It is a cruel fact that a lot of brainy women earn their living, but the sensible ones let men do it for them. Actually, what women know about men doesn't amount to much, but what they suspect makes up for it. If a husband could actually do all those things his wife suspects he does, he'd be eager to extol the joys of double-blessedness.

As I mentioned earlier, a wise woman will never insist on prying into every mood a man happens to be in; when a man lapses into a gloomy but meditative silence, it's always a mistake for a woman to intrude with: "What are you thinking about, dear—you're not mad, are you?" The same things hold true for you girls, because it just doesn't pay to be too open with yourself. When you reveal everything to your man, you deny him the right of discovery.

The real reason that women are difficult to communicate with is that the only time they think clearly is while they're washing their hair.

When women try to make themselves indispensable to men, it is nothing but their secret demand for power. But when a woman places herself between a man and his work, constantly interrupting or distracting him, she weakens her position in his life. If a woman disturbs her man's peace of mind, she mars his concentration and therefore jeopardizes his career. Women should take care to be more practical and prudent. After all, if a woman jeopardizes a man's career, he won't be able to support her in the manner she yearns for.

> *My two ex-wives are the*
> *only women I know who*
> *made a brilliant marriage.*

A Woman's Physique

A woman's physique is the key to her entire being. Most men are attracted to women purely on the basis of appearance, so if a woman doesn't pay attention to her body, nobody else will, either. A beautiful woman will always be desired by all men, and, consequently, she herself will desire all men. So as a wife, an authentic superfox is more trouble than she's worth. The way she crosses her legs is a gesture smooth and exact, like an expensive instrument being folded into its felt-lined box. She always costs a man everything he owns, psychologically and monetarily.

This section is not devoted to those of you out there in your threadbare rayon all-weather jammies, seething with indecision and despondency, anxiously checking out those tiny but deepening crow's feet at the corner of your flirty-flirty eyes. No, I'd rather deal with you girls who still have something left to barter with, those of you who don't feel that your only survival kit is between your legs.

Face it, some poor clunky, chunky babes just can't make it with their off-beat gait; they lurch through life in a concave slouch like the Queen Elizabeth with a bad case of shifting cargo. They walk as if their chain-mail chastity belt chafes their main bearing as they go clomping through life like an unemployed sorceress.

It helps if a woman is so beautiful that she could start a real estate boom in Death Valley. I once knew a nifty who was so sumptuously endowed that strong men would cling to lampposts and sob aloud as she jounced by. In fact, every man within a hundred yards would whimper and paw the ground when her ripply walk sashayed her down that boulevard of broken bras. She was such a natural beauty that her attitude toward cosmetic mudpacks was, "They may be OK, but they haven't done much for hogs."

You girls remember, it's easier to walk the straight and narrow if you're built that way, and if you're developing a few hashmarks on your aging torso, remember that a woman is only as old as she looks to a man who likes to look at her. And that applies even if you're in the springtime of your senility with most of your faculties impaired.

One of the incentives to marriage is the desire for property, which is a subdivision of the craving for power. To the typical woman, that Empress of Intrigue, marriage is a fabulous source of revenue; a husband is mighty valuable property. And she is worth plenty to him—after all, no other domestic animal is so useful, or so greatly gratifies the vanity of the owner. I know one guy who deliberately married a brilliant wife because he prefers his nagging with a little culture.

A girl who has a figure that doesn't need support will always find a man to support her, and it. For as she brandishes her bosom and lullaby body in moves that are guaranteed to pivot the passerby, this glorious blob of girlhood will find that he will eagerly feed and clothe her until that flaccid, globoid day when her shape becomes epidemic and begins to spread. So, girls, flaunt what Mother Nature gave you before Father Time takes it away.

Women age in a peculiar way; thirty years of passionate romance makes her look like a combat ruin, but thirty years of stolid marriage makes her look like a public building, all ivy-covered and dedicated. Her husband is kind, truthful, considerate, helpful, courteous, understanding, loyal . . . and a complete bore. She's a Capricorn and he's a Wino. She indulges in a little creative adultery and her sole remaining erotic fantasy, her one secret, powerful yearning is to fondle John Wayne's saddlehorn. At one time, their vintage relationship was in such dire straits that their marriage counselor made house calls. Her phlegmatic husband isn't too thrilled, either, at this lengthy marriage of mutual attrition. But it's his own fault; they got married shortly after the H-bomb was perfected; at that time, he figured they'd all be wiped out in a few months anyway.

> *The trouble with women is—they*
> *inspire a man to do great things,*
> *and then they keep him from doing them.*

Further Observations on Fat

I don't like fat; not at all. Most men feel the same way, particularly if the fat is on a woman who used to be slender. There are few things more depressing than a woman sadly regarding her ballooning thighs, and wondering if she'll have to crank her porker pants up her massive legs with a chain-hoist.

From the day a woman weighs 160 pounds, the chief excitement in her life consists in spotting women who are fatter than she is. This is a degrading existence, and you know you're fat when you step out of the shower and you're profoundly relieved that the mirror is all fogged up and you can't see yourself.

If she's a relative, you introduce the fat babe by saying, "I want you to meet my own flesh and flab."

I hate to see a woman who has let herself go, one who has a figure like a melted candle. I know a woman who had her appendix removed; she was so fat, her doctor had to operate with a bread knife. She had a bell bottom, with a residual rump. This is the kind of woman who, if she were a singer, her only role would be Madame Butterball. She's so fat that she'd have to buckle on a corset before she could squeeze into her Japanese kimono.

You girls must remember that obesity is a mental state, a disease brought on by boredom and disappointment. So if you have become a vast waddle of womanhood, read on.

> *Most calorie fighters spend*
> *too much time fraternizing*
> *with the enemy.*

There are few things more depressing than a woman sadly regarding her ballooning thighs and wondering if she'll have to crank her porker pants up her massive legs with a chain-hoist.

Dietary Alternatives
or
Practicing Girth Control

This section is for you girls who are overweight and are thick and tired of it. I once knew a chubby, moon-faced sow who always carried her calorie book with her—she liked to have something to read with her chocolate dessert. So instead of force-feeding yourselves on bon-bons and fudgecake, washed down with extra-thick milkshakes, you can exercise a little self-discipline and follow the dietary guidelines that I have found will cure you of excessive eating. So if you have more chins than a Chinese phone directory, join me now, but note that any woman who thinks she can hold her husband with her cooking should remember that he wasn't eating a sandwich when he proposed.

Let's begin with dessert, since this is the one course that seems to add the most pounds the fastest. Instead of gorging yourself on French pastry, try a bowl of enchilada ice cream, with a tasty Luden's coughdrop on top. Determine to fight off every excess pound as if it were a political opponent.

A plastic cup of sardine sherbet is always a big hit for dessert among the nautical set, especially if it's followed by a side order of candied grunion and salty remarks. If she is still fat, don't put her down, pal; slip an arm as far around her waist as possible and mutter hoarsely, "I love the very ground that trembles under your feet."

Incidentally, I have a tip for you ladies who are feeling wide-in-the-hide but who insist on baking your own low-cal desserts: Remember that the cake is done when your knife blade breaks off in it. If you decide to avoid dreary baking, you can always try a liquid dessert, like a Nujol rickey, or a Snarol float.

There are many nutritious entrees: Baked loin of gopher, rabbit stroganoff, or creamed caterpillar, which is easy on the digestive tract, if you can get it down without being intimidated by your enzymes' anguished screams. The same holds true for pickled parakeet feet, or a chilled bowl of albatross fetlocks. If you favor something a trifle more exotic, you might try a parboiled kangaroo pouch, marinated in Midol (very relaxing). Of course, don't overdo. What's the good of keeping your figure if you don't have the strength to move it around? That was once said by a girl who was awfully unhappy about being fat. In fact, the only time she was happy at all was when she was eating.

Vegetables are always a bore unless prepared correctly. That's why a cauliflower soufflé or turnips a la mode must be given close attention, and are best served with something gamey, like baked pancreas of stud buzzard. You could buy that desperate new reducing pill—it paralyzes your mouth so you *can't* eat. Of course worrying makes you lose weight, unless it's your weight that you're worrying about.

If you've been on a diet for two months and all you've lost is your temper, try any combination of the following exotica: Marinated moray eel, beaver broth, and minced wolverine giblets smothered in curried praying mantis; this makes a delectable combination, as does teriyaki toadstools over armadillo viscera laced with fermented Granola.

If you're feeling queasy, an unguentine omelette will soothe your viscera. But if you're feeling spry and chipper and you need something saucy, try pigsnout hollandaise with creosote gravy.

If your husband is one of those safari-oriented hunters, you might try prime rib of baby zebra, or a broiled jowl of pygmy hippo, or even ossified antler of scimitar-horned gazelle.

Whatever you do though, girls, don't follow the terrible example of an overweight neighbor of mine. She was so fat that when she took off her girdle, she spread out like a bale of hay after the retaining wires were snipped. Unfortunately, she liked a simple, nourishing lunch of clear broth made from formaldehyde, lemon peel, and bourbon, all of which she washed down with a fistful of diet pills. And she lost a lot of weight. In fact, when I last saw her, she weighed 94 pounds, including her coffin.

> *The best way to get rid of weight*
> *Is to leave it on your heaping plate,*
> *(because)*
> *The most familiar table spread*
> *Is seen on people, not on bread.*

Addiction to Adornment

Most women are hooked on clothes, and while it's not true that clothes and women are inseparable, clothes are vital to their morale. (I once heard a woman say, "I'd commit suicide if I had the proper clothes.")

But this information is not directed at those women who like to nibble the tortured cuticle from their chafed and reddened, careworn fingers. I am talking to the girl who wears a bottom-less shawl contrived from an old-fashioned checkerboard quilt, handed down to her from great grandma who rolled an elderly looter for it when she was a campfollower during Sherman's retreat to the sea, and she always wears such a wild red-splattered tie that she looks like the victim of a mad tracheot-omist. A girl like this not only displays a lively, fearless imagination, but she has history and heredity on her side, as well as an off-center, plunging mustard plaster.

You can really tell a lot about a girl by the clothes she's wearing, and, if you're lucky enough to be there, the manner in which she puts them on. What would a man think, for example, of a woman who hauls a threadbare, coffee-stained shift out of a bureau drawer and slips it over her head without first re-moving that cigarette dangling from her lips? And you must realize early on that the difference between a camisole and a casserole is the kind of chick you put into it.

Ballance's Law of Appearances—the best costume is one that *reveals* little but *promises* much. And a sensible girl is not as sensible as she looks, because a sensible girl has more sense than to look sensible.

It is advisable for you girls to avoid wearing inflammable pantyhose; I know a dancer who was gyrating so vigorously the other night that her pantyhose caught fire, singeing her somewhat, and incinerating her otherwise. Better just to wear recycled sealed-beam skivvies with limp elastic; if they are throwaway panties, print your phone number inside to stimulate your social life.

There is nothing phonier than a rich hippie, a woman fanning the flames of frustration, sitting around in a tie-dyed T-shirt and cut-off caftan trying to achieve forlorn waifhood. She spends hours back-combing her hair and dragging her new jeans around the pool on the abrasive concrete to age them, and thus instantly garb herself in counter-culture tatters. This is known as the David Copperfield Caper, and has Charles Dickens fidgeting in his sarcophagus.

Image plays an important part in a woman's concept of herself, and clothes contribute to that image. Scrunchy Monday morning togs feed her fantasy of tawdry charm plus a freshly plucked upper lip, and in the afternoon she slips into her funkadelic scooterskirt and biodegradable blazer covered with astrological pornopatches that help her project raunchy, radical chic. She is convinced that the only timely clothes are products of either cultural lag or future shock. I know one doubleknit doll who digs wearing contrasting outfits—a green velvet-lined sealskin vest edged with gold embroidery, chamois gloves that button up to her armpits, a pokebonnet of covered-wagon calico, and knickerbockers of interwoven watercress which stretches all the way from her knickers clear down to her bocker. Underneath this rig she wears utilitarian panties made from newspaper comic strips. You should see the spot Dick Tracy's in now.

A return to natural clothing, or lack of clothing, is the thing now for Miss Swaggery Hotstrut. Homespun bib-overalls smudged with nature's own plankton are the rage; and don't forget that new two-piece outfit: Gossamer spats. This is known as "understated elegance." This way, she's more appealing than when she wears baggy pants with all the fun taken out of them. For some women, the no-bra fashion is a big letdown, and if that hip new brass bra becomes a fad, a lot of girls will get their gongs bonged.

I once met a girl who was so smitten by her image of herself as a skier that when she was smote she kept her tiny calloused feet in a pair of gilded ski-boots with metallic laces. She wore her hair up in a loose knot in the middle of her rounded back, and held it in place with a loop of solid gold baling wire. And she prowled the beginners' slope as if she were concealing the Holy Grail in her triangular slalom . . . an effect achieved by wearing her boyfriend's balsa-wood codpiece.

Après-ski, she wore an authentic French Foreign Legionnaire dress uniform and carried a corroded quart canteen of natural spring water from Walden Pond. She is fully aware that when a girl is noted for her *warmth,* it seldom comes from what she's *wearing.*

But deliver us from women who, when 60, dress like 22, for even though their hearts are young, their figures may have slipped a rung. This is Ballance's Contour Quatrain.

If, however, a woman is bountifully endowed, she should not wear one of those new bosom-flattening tank-tops, because her breasts are an endangered species and should never be bound down; it'd be like confining a tiger in a bird cage. And I urge you girls to avoid those unisex styles of androgynous chic. Stay positive, stay healthy, stay fashionable, but please stay women. Remember Ballance's Accoutrement Axiom—What you *are* speaks so loudly, we men don't really care what you're *wearing.* After all, the most fetching costume is just your skin.

> *If you want to know next year's styles in women's clothes, look at this year's prostitutes.*

Gifts, Fun and Games,
and Interpersonal Highjinks

If we men knew what was actually going on in the minds of women, we'd be a hundred times more aggressive and amorous. Think of all the gasoline that would be saved if we men knew what you girls were really thinking.

Most men fail to realize that a woman's greatest asset is a man's imagination, and that a Sunday School face usually harbors Saturday night ideas.

Even though the quickest way to a woman's heart is through the side door of a Ferrari, a few gifts can be helpful. If she dips snuff, a genuine brass cuspidor will enchant her. Or if she's an outdoor girl (a beast) give her an army boondocks pocket knife which contains 12 stainless steel tools, including cutting and sawing blade, can opener, scissors, fish-scaler, nail file, cork-screw, and lock-pick. And as a thoughtful gesture of considera-tion for her girlish gullet, give her a carton of Linda Lovelace Throat Lozenges.

Sometimes age can be a factor in gift-giving, so here's a nifty way to tell a woman's age: If she urges you to cuddle her for a candy bar, she's 7 to 12; for 2 comic books, she's 12 to 14; for a hamburger and a movie, she's 14 to 16; for a drive-in and popcorn, she's 16 to 18; for a dance and flowers, she's 18 to 21; for jewelry and clothes, she's 21 to 30; for a 5th of gin, she's 30 to 40; for trading stamps, she's 40 to 50; and finally, for a smile or a nod, she's 50 to 60; for a nudge, she's 60 on up.

It's the solemn truth that the best years of a *woman's* life are figured in *man* hours, and where adultery is a *stimulant* to men, it is generally a *sedative* to women. A man looks forward, while a woman remembers, even though there is nothing more har-rowing than a freshly divorced woman who is anxiously mo-bilized again for love.

It is written as Ballance's Doctrine of Decoration that women should be worn like a boutonniere, to add to a man's look of distinction, and to contribute to his aura of well-being. A woman should be delightful to pluck and easy to replace, she should be put on with pleasure, removed without pain, and remembered with hormonal nostalgia. But the two most aggravating feminine attributes that cause the greatest exasperation are, (a) that she is irresistible, and (b) that she is irreplaceable. You wonder how irresistible and irreplaceable? Listen, I'm on the air from 10 to 3 p.m., Monday through Saturday, and I see my midday audience as a WOMAN, not to be taken by storm, but to be wooed gently and lovingly. When I take calls from my dollbabies, I am reminded minute by minute that those listeners out there are not just disembodied voices; they comprise ONE woman, yearning to be seduced.

Of course you know that a woman never really *makes* a fool out of a man; she merely *directs* the performance. Also, I don't know anything better than a woman if you want to spend money where it'll show. And remember that there is only one way to handle a woman—but nobody knows what it is.

When they're alone, women love to fantasize, and most of them actually carry out these fantasies, while lying spreadeagled in front of a fireplace, making ferocious love with Frenzied Vigor (the gatekeeper) arms and legs reciprocating briskly. Breathing fire and moaning low, she loves to cavort in the nude before her mirror, whirling voluptuously in a blur of joy, spraying the front room with a Martini atomizer, laying plans to get polarized in as ladylike a fashion as possible, and wondering if it's really true that cucumber brine disguises the aroma of gin, because rain or shine, baby, it's always pouring at your house, right?

You house-bound girls love to tilt an earthenware crock up to your tremulous rosebuds and decant pre-war tranquility through same; if that's your number, do it. You've earned it. We men are forever indebted to women; first for life itself, and then for making life worth living. So don't commit the ultimate gaffe of holding back; remain avid for life. It is engraved as Ballance's Hedonistic Formulation that it's far better to feel remorse for what you've done than to feel regret for what you failed to do.

There is no man so assured that he cannot be made to feel slightly oafish if a subtle and complex woman really puts her mind to it, especially if she likes to make violent love to Kabuki chords. It can really put a guy uptight if a woman comes at him all twitching with desire, like a wild animal in its first exposure to love or gunfire; she slithers around the room like an insolent incarnation of sin. Such aggressiveness will always geld a timid lover, but will detonate guffaws from a bold stud.

Trying to change certain customs is like trying to move Catalina two feet to the west; and the body of unwritten regulations governing behavior between men and women has all the attributes of an immovable object. I'm afraid it's a mass of ancient law, prejudice, habit, and 19th-century morality, whose peaks and valleys are permanently obscured in the mists of historical absurdity and mind-boggling prudish confusion. But study these pages, girls, and let me help you preserve your right to be cherished. Let me hook up my book to the pleasure terminal of your brain.

Never marry a man in order to change him. Remember Ballance's Nuptial Maxim—human nature cannot be altered by being haltered. And men—to be happy with a woman, you must love her a lot, and try not to understand her at all; and never forget to assure a woman that she is unlike any other woman in the world; which she is certain to believe. After doing that, you may proceed to deal with her as you would any other woman.

What first *attracts* a man to a woman never *binds* him to her, because a woman is like a fire; she goes out if she is unattended. And if she is the complaining sort, always whining about random aches, just cure her by telling her that such complaints are the first symptoms of old age. And that reminds me—I still can't figure out why Doris Day refused to elope with me when I met her at a party the other night. All I said was, "After all, my dear, you're not getting any younger."

So, sweetheart, if you're a crumpled adult, badgered by burdens, harried by time, made cautious by too many collisions with an unrelenting Destiny, watch what you say to your guy at a party. Remember Ballance's Stern Festive Edict: *A woman who makes fun of her husband in public no longer loves him.* If your marriage has deteriorated into polite superficialities and stagnant compromise, if your marriage is closing in upon itself like a flower withdrawing from the sun, and you suddenly realize that your posture of wifely devotion is only economic dependency, better check the wind-chill factor of your heart. If you are sure it's all over, say to yourself, "OK, I've lost interest in the cheese—now how do I get out of the trap?" But don't be impulsive; after all, many women get *even* with their husbands by *staying married* to them.

I'll never forget one night when one of my ex-wives plopped down next to me in the den while I was watching television; she asked shakily if I didn't feel that perhaps the excitement had gone out of our marriage, and I whispered, "We'll discuss it during the next commercial." She deserved it, though. She refused to listen with rapt admiration and constant applause to tapes of my shows. But she did teach me one of the priceless skills of matrimony—the ability to listen without hearing.

Let me finish this chapter by emphasizing that I know it's absurd to pretend that a man cannot love the same woman always; it would be just as plausible to pretend that a good artist needs several violins to execute a complex piece of music. It's just that I personally prefer to urge many women to: "Rub me with rosin and call me your beau."

> *A woman would rather marry*
> *a poor provider any time,*
> *than a poor listener.*

Chapter Nine
Drugs, Suicide, and Death

Drugs and Suicide

Drugs and suicide are both means of running away from reality. The only difference between them is that one is temporary and the other is permanent. They are both destructive and meaningless, and should have no place in your life. Our ultimate future is Death anyway, so why hurry it? And there's no more pathetic sight than kids' suffering from post-LSD feeblemindedness. These past few years, drugs have become the divorce decree between generations.

When people are stoned into a state of sustained paranoia, disaster follows. Disaster alters your plans, and dope alters your mind. Only fools slowly kill themselves auditioning for that deadly movie, "Pride of the Junkies," in which they play a losing role, and wind up on a slab with their big toes tied together.

When you shoot up with anything, it's like sniping at yourself. Ignore all that bogus mind-expanding myth; ignore anything that damages your brain cells, anything whose most benign side-effects are hepatitis and malnutrition. Why waste time hallucinating and crippling your mind permanently? The real effect of drugs is to neutralize life. Dopers don't have the guts to do something positive about the world they put down. So they get stoned and hope that when they awaken, things will be different. Well, all that's different is their brains, which have been irreparably damaged. Most acid-heads are loners and losers, with few friends and fewer accomplishments. They scream that they want *freedom,* yet they tie themselves up completely with drugs.

Choking on their over-stuffed but dysfunctional egos, so-called growth-seekers have only re-discovered and reworked the old maxim that one must lose oneself. Some of these encounter facilitators urge participants to, "Lose your mind and come to your senses." I object to that; I say that the senses you come to won't be worth the mind, especially if you've already blown it on drugs. If you want to witness the new century's arrival, don't let yourself be captured by the *give-me-librium-or-give-me-meth-syndrome,* don't sign on with the International Order of Junkies, Pushers, Dealers, and Dangerously Deluded Dropouts, and end up in Zonk City.

Face it, chums, drug addicts are deliberately letting their lives slip away; they're all emaciated and self-martyred, and they're dramatizing themselves into an early grave. Don't get involved in that lethal idiocy. Life is exciting—all you need to do is be willing to accept it and seek out its pleasures. Life is a series of haphazards—improvisational theater in the round. It'll give you a natural high without methadone popsicles.

I will admit that I have thought of killing myself; but only with kindness. Or, if I really got depressed I might consider doing it with a tidal wave. Because it's the final form of escapism, suicide is the sincerest kind of criticism given to life. You really have to be a depressing believer in pessimistic philosophies in order to do yourself in. Why choose to become toast of the week for the crematorium? It's mighty black out there in eternity, and it lasts a long time.

Don't bleep yourself out of existence; we are already born with a death sentence, and are only given a brief reprieve. Why deliberately try to extricate yourself from life? Be afraid of nothing, for every man's life ends the same way. The good life is available to those who have the wit to search it out, not to those who become preoccupied with morbid death fantasies, like suicide.

Another consideration is the threat of failure, and the embarrassment you'll no doubt suffer. I knew a DJ who, in a fit of depression, threw himself into a vat of Preparation H, and he shrank into the size of a kumquat; it took the morticians five days to wipe that pucker off his face. Imagine how his family must have felt during the "viewing" of his open casket. Probably relieved.

Suicide is rarely a laughing matter, and I'm sure that the successful participants find it less than exhilarating. Killing yourself is a major loss of your cool. It is a confession of failure; of terrible guilt. Death by your own hand is the ultimate dropout, the greatest disrespect for individual self-esteem, and the supreme example of a total loss of control.

Don't commit suicide; in the measureless realm of time, that Great Delicatessen Keeper in the Sky already cuts our slice of eternity mighty thin.

> *Never abandon life. There*
> *is a way out of everything,*
> *except Death.*

Life and Death

The only way to avoid escapist fantasies induced by drugs and thoughts of suicide, is to discover the art of living; the art of living is to stalk the earth like a prince, scattering apples wherever you go. The art of dying is to finish your own apple just at the right moment and say, "All right, that's enough—the rest of these apples are for you to enjoy at my graveside."

Once you're caught by Death, the most relentless of all pursuers, you're forever under the sod. And as for immortality, I refuse to worry about more than one world at a time. Death is the central factor of life, and the simple comprehension of this fact alters your perspective. Death is the ultimate teardrop; life, without knowledge of its pleasures can simply become a line of work that always leads toward a distant and tragic conclusion.

Life is a moving sliver of time between what was and what will be; it gives no guarantee of its length, so time is priceless, no matter how old you are. You only have one life to live and you only live it once; you can't start over again. When someone we know dies, we are suddenly hit by visions of our own mortality, so don't fritter away your life. Man is foredoomed to aging, changes, and ultimate death, which is essentially a sound sleep undisturbed by foolish dreams. I knew one of my marriages was finished when she gazed speculatively at me one morning and asked, "Just *when* do I start living longer than you?"

Sometimes people actually look forward to death, provided, of course, it is followed by a fine funeral. I knew one actress who, if she'd known what a terrific funeral she was going to have, would have died years earlier.

Death is total cellular disintegration, while life is like a heavy crust we're walking on; we think things are all right and then suddenly there is a crack and we see that all-consuming fire raging underneath.

The single most important thing I've learned is that I'm going to die. For once you accept your own death, all of a sudden, you are free to live, and you remind yourself constantly that *TIME* is the one irreplaceable commodity.

It is always revealing to yourself if you figure out what is really most important to you—not what society tells you is important, but what you, in your moments alone, *know* is important to you. At this stage of my life the ONLY things I care about are my health, my work, my sons, women, reading, and money. One of the most effective ways to bring everything into focus is to write your own epitaph. Mine will read: For a lifetime he thought he was gripping the microphone, but at the end he learned it was the other way around.

There I go lying to you. There won't be any headstone, and so there'll be no epitaph. (An epitaph is a belated advertisement for a line of goods that has been permanently discontinued.) I have officially donated my body to UCLA MEDICAL CENTER, so that eventually, I'll be bobbing around in a cask of brine and, who knows, you might even end up with one of my favorite corneas.

All I had to do was attend a couple of funerals and watch aghast at the perpetually bereaved look on the undertaker's face . . . his expression was one of crushed but competent unction as he offered coo's of condolence. (He later told me he became an undertaker because he "liked working with people.") I decided that wasn't for me; anyway, it'd be nice to contribute a random part of my body to someone after I'm through with it . . . but not one moment before, so stop gazing at me speculatively as if you're taking inventory.

Anyone who thinks you cannot change the past
has never read an obituary.

Chapter Ten
Bill Ballance's
Annotated Bibliography
and Grudging
Acknowledgments

And now, with a blithe display of venality that would have done credit to P. T. Barnum, I remind you that the purpose of this book is to exonerate the innocent, prosecute the guilty, resolve history since the dawn of time, and make a lot of money. That's right; I plan for this outrageously readable book (now in its fifth printing because I print very slowly) to make me wealthy beyond the dreams of Croesus—Carl Croesus, the notorious slumlord who owns my apartment building, Crestfallen Manor.

Harsh reviewers are therefore warned to be enthusiastic and generous lest I cast a malevolent hex on them, for it is written as Ballance's Prose Postulate that criticism is the lowest form of art, that a critic is a humanoid who seeks to do something creative by criticizing creation. He's like a eunuch; he's aware of exciting things going on around him, but he is unequipped by nature to take part. Wilfrid Sheed, of course, is the exception. I'm not really afraid of critics, just . . . well, apprehensive; so I remind myself that the permanence of any book is fixed, not by friendly or hostile criticism, but by that book's specific gravity,

by its intrinsic importance, by its impact on the receptive mind of man.

Reminiscent of a mid-nineteenth century "Commonplace" or "Thoughtbook," made up of clippings and quotes favored over the years by the compiler, my peeping tome is bristling with recycled axioms you might recognize, plus fragrant fragments from obscure journals, for, indeed, all work and no plagiarism makes a dull book. Having been a voracious reader all my life (Velma Voracious is my favorite historian; she was a Confederate spy whose memoirs were entitled, *1862 AND ALL THAT or HOW I SHILLY-SHALLIED AT SHILOH WITH A LOVE-SICK SENTRY WHO FELL ASLEEP ON HIS SWORD*). I've absorbed countless random shafts, some with hollies on them.

So with that feeble copout, let me state that it's only fair to credit the following unwitting contributors:

How to Take Slight but Pleasant Comfort from Small Vengeances as You Grow Older by Lawrence Welk

Planned Pantryhood—A Cookbook for People with Bad Teeth by Mike Roy

Easy Steps to Terminal Gluttony by George Sanders

Black is the Color of My True Love's Late Date by Stephen Foster

Will the Preparation-H Bomb Shrink the World of Tomorrow? by Nostradamus

Apes Talk Dirty—Little Known Anthropological Facts About Primates by Margaret Mead

Fringy Love in the Back of a Surrey by Jenny Jerome

How Mae West Was Won by Rex Reed

The Boss Tweed Guide to Absolute Corruption by his Mighty Proud Great-Grandson, Harris Tweed

Each Dawn I Die by Ralph Story

The Wonderful World of Botulism or A Woman's Place Is in the Oven by Eve Curie

Did Mother Goose the Ancient Mariner? by the Brothers Grimm

My Fight with German Measles by Dr. Werner Von Braunose

There Is no Lunar Gravity—The Moon Sucks. Ibid.

"101 Useful Objects a Resourceful Boy Can Make Out of Human Skin," from *The Tanganyika Scout Manual*

My Supermom From Double-Motherland by Oedipus Rexford

Droll Ascerbity among Court Bailiffs I Have Known, With a Complete Judicial Analysis of Their Coruscating Wit by Chief Justice John Marshall

How to Avoid Slipping into Lifelong Obscurity by Judge Joseph Crater

When We Did a Show at the Molokai Leper Colony Our Rating Dropped Off by Hudson and Landry

Sexual Drive from Six till Ten and from Ten till Midnight by Bernard Baruch

The Day I Hiked the Appalachian Trail with Kate Smith and Lived by Mamma Cass

How I Broke the Oatmeal Habit by Tuesday Weld, as confessed to the Osmond Brothers

Braceros We Have Known and Smuggled for a Profit by Cheech and Chong

The Romance of Cold Sores by Dr. Harry Herpes

Avarice in Action or The Rich Get Richer and the Poor Get Plastic Drapes by John D. Rockefeller IV

Those Puritans Weren't the Only Ones Punished in Stocks by Bernie Cornfeld

Common Household Insects and How to Use Them as Flavoring by Jane Goodall

What Prominent Television Host Frankly Admits that He Can Neither Read nor Write? by David Susskind

Mexico on Five Toilets a Day by Ambrose Bierce

An Hilarious Treasury of Human Abnormalities, Including Personal Hygiene Problems of Siamese Twins by Minnie the Mermaid

I Was a Groupie for John Philip Sousa by Madame Wanda Landowska

Is Bering Straight? by Walter Hickel

The Double Negative versus the Single Shot or When Your Cup Runneth Over Lick it off the Bar by Dean Martin
   (reprinted in *The Betty Cooker Crockbook*)

Why the Hip Set in London Considered Lord Nelson a Trafalgar Square and the Real Reason Anne Boleyn Lost Her Head when She Called Henry VIII a Fat Bum by Sir Winston Churchill

Hollywood's Most Eligible Bachelors and When They'll Be Free Again by Rona Barrett

The Night I Punched Billy Graham in the Mouth by Dale Carnegie

Selective Promiscuity for the Horny Housewife by Truman Capote

The Real Story of the Little Big Horn by Al Hirt

Cornish Game Hens I Have Whirled on my Rotisserie by Victor Borge

Shoplifting Is a Crime by Ali Baba

My Hat Is Hard—Confessions of a Construction Worker by "C" (for Cement)

Liverwurst Through the Ages or Why Cookbooks Have Stirring Chapters by Betty Crocker

Better Things for Better Living Through Chicanery by Jim Pendergast, Sr.

Train Your Grapevines with a Whip and Chair by Ernesto Gallo

Dumbbell People in a Barbell World by Jack LaLanne

I Went for a Tramp in the Woods, But He Escaped by Henry David Thoreau

Burt Reynolds and the Mysterious Gila Bend Heiffer by Sarah Miles

You Too Can Mould a Mighty Larynx by Tiny Tim

The Truth about John Audubon's Cockatoo by His Senior Aviary Attendant

The Charlton Heston Nobody Knows by Ben Hur

Does the Jumbo Jet Eat Its Young? by Howard Hughes

I've Fallen Into Something and I Hope It's Love or It's Hard to Be in Seventh Heaven When You've Been Married Six Times Before by Lana Turner

A Woman's Guide to Gambling or How to Influence Dice with Tears, a sequel to *How One Deals Blackjack while Wearing Long White Gloves* by Grace Kelly

What You've Always Wanted to Know about Your Stomach but Didn't Have the Guts to Ask by Dr. Vernon Viscera

To Err Is Human, To Forgive, Supine or The Night Has a Thousand Girls by Xaviera

Hitler's Beast—The Story of Eva Braun and Her Magic Lampshade by Martin Bormann

John Muir's Crush on Teddy Roosevelt or What Really Happened at Yosemite by John J. Pershing

How I Drive My Car with One Hand and My Girl Crazy with the Other by Porfirio Rubirosa

I am Joe's Hemorrhoid by Rafael Sabatini

The Suicide's Home Companion—A Gauche Guide to Eternity by The Staff at Jiffy Embalming School, Home of WHAMO Formaldehyde

What the Well-Bred Blackmailer Should Write by Gary Owens

The Freudian Significance of Clicking Your Lover's Certs by Maureen Reagan

Imus in the Morning Meets Ballance in the Flesh by The Brothers Sarnoff

Robots Have No Guts by The Houston Space Center Command Module Senior Char-Ladies

How to Be Happily Married (Science Fiction) by Mickey Rooney

I Fell In Love with My Footlocker by General George Custer

Is Doing the Frug Really Good for the Metatarsal Arch? by Fred Astaire

Read It and Gasp by Samuel Pepys

How to Grow Sunflowers in Your Laundry Chute by Lynn and Joel Rapp (Mother Earth)

Training a Baby by the Book Is a Good Idea, But You Need a Different Book for Each Baby by Pauline Paregoric, Dr. Spock's Aged Nanny

The Only Thing We Have to Fear Is Eleanor Roosevelt by Alice Longworth as gleefully cackled to Bella Abzug

My Secret Files—Confessions of a Manicurist by Becky Thatcher

How to Catch the Bride's Bouquet and the Best Man's Eye by Selma Diamond

The Brutal War of Northern Aggression by General Robert E. Lee (formerly *An Unbiased History of the War Between the States from a Southern Point of View*)

The Things You Told Masters and Johnson Are the Things You Should Have Told Me by Oscar Wilde

The Decline and Fall of My Bosom by Raquel Welch

It's Only a Shanty in Old Shanty-Town by Conrad Hilton

How Twiggy Overcame Her Obesity Problem by Mia Farrow

I Wake Up Every Morning with a Heartache by Dick Whittington

"How to Cure Rampaging Halitosis with Acupuncture" from Spicy Mechanics

What Every Woman Wants by Warren Beatty

The Truth about Migrating Tree-Toads by John Audubon

I Married My Baby-Sitter; The Poignant Story of a Young Man's Love For an Older Woman by David Cassidy

Some Do's and Don'ts for the Woman about to be Executed by Marie Antoinette

The Ten Best Ways to Serve Your Fellow Man by The Donner Summit Five

Rebecca of Sunnybrook Prison Farm by Harriet Beecher Stowe

How I Turned Woman Suffrage into a Profitable Hobby by Gloria Steinem

Aesop's Foibles by Dr. David Rubens

Good News for Molecules by Albert Einstein

Sex Without Love is Better Than Nothing by Frank Sinatra

Curdle Up with a Good Mystery by Ross Macdonald

Science Fiction is the Folklore of the Future by Isaac Asimov

No Man is an Island by Jack Catalina

How to Get the Most Money out of Your Patients without Actually Treating Them Hippocrates

A Golden Treasury of Early America's Simple Tapestries and Elaborate Guile by Willis Watergate

Other Publications, Treatises, Dissertations, Pamphlets, and Tracts from which Many Book-cerpts Have Been Made by Bill Ballance Because He Wrote Them in the First Place:

Support the Fortune 500—Learn to Tolerate the Whims of the Solvent

How to Stave Off Embarrassing Premature Jubilation

An Anthology of the Nation's Finest Muggings

I Forged the Dead Sea Scrolls

Power Tools I Have Owned and Been Maimed By

What to Do if You Strangle on a Hairball

I Thought I Had Wall-To-Wall Carpeting till One Day I Scrubbed the Floor

How to Strengthen Your Character without Actually Going to Jail

It's No Disgrace to Be Poor, But It Might As Well Be

What to Do When the Recession Hits Your Gums

I Was a Grammar-School Celibate

Peter Rabbit's First Affair

How a Swiss Bell-Ringer Got Tangled Up in His Rope and Tolled Himself Off

Pennywise and Woman Simple

The Collected Letters of Our Alphabet

How to Amortize Your Children

The Five Little Peppers Go Through the Mill

I Fought the Man-Eating Grunion and Survived, Thanks to Slippery Fingers

Love Letters from Ma Kettle to Fidel Castro

Mary Todd Lincoln, Secret Surfer

The Rise and Fall of the Third Curtain

Never Be Ashamed of What You Are—I'm Not Ashamed of What You Are or Self-Help Books Are Aimed at the Reader Who Is Beyond Help in the First Place

The Hunchback Who Knew a Lot of Dames—With a Typical Hollywood Ending in Which the Hero Chokes to Death on a Tranquilizer

Success Has Turned More Heads than Halitosis

Is Peoria Burning? Only if We're Lucky (published by Charnel House)

One Thousand Ways to Prepare Yogurt; (Sequel) One More Thing You Can Do with Yogurt

Bail I Have Forfeited

What to Do until the Termite Exterminator Comes

The American Mother and Her Victims

I Found My Thrill on Hadley Rille

The Wonderful World of Ringworm

How to Ball without a Chain

You, Too, Can Become Catnip to Women

The Private Life of a Hollywood Chihuahua

Perpetuating My Pearls for Profit in Peckish Pamphlets

Power—How to Seize It and Enjoy It

How to Make Round Trips as a Sky-Diver

My Plans for 1984—Winning the Presidency on the STAG Ticket: Straight-Talking American Government

You Can't Judge a Book By Its Author

How to Become a Tremendously Successful Scapegoat

Why Girls Go Wrong—And Where to Find Them

Ready, Willing, and Disabled By Love

The World Is Our Polluted Oyster

Scrofulous Boarding Houses I Have Known

The Girl with the Take-Out Brain

Basic Principles of Marathon Leapfrog

Are You Really Being Kept, or Just Detained?

New Uses for Old Friends

Potty-Training Self-Taught

Proper English for You and I or I Seen Good Books Ruined by Pretentious Syntax

How to Ski while Your Hips Are in Traction

Why I Would Like to Be a Siamese Twin of Linda Lovelace and Where I'd Like to Be Joined to Her for Life

Fads, Follies, and Delusions of Dry-Ice Sculpturing

Smalltown Girls with Big Illusions

SEAR—Society for the Emasculation of American Radio

Malignant Birthmark Decals—The New Craze

Why Senile Strippers Bump Themselves Off

Wartime Service with a British Thermal Unit

Show Me a Policeman Who Flogs Those Drums and I'll Show You a Cop on the Beat

Spiffy Remarks

"I love Bill Ballance's writing so much, I'd be more than willing to illustrate his books; I'd love to design the jacket and write a poetic preface—hell, I'd even chew wood pulp to provide the paper."—*Emily Dickinson*

"Monsieur Ballance is able to capture in verbal nets the irridescent fish of fascinating thought."—*Guy de Maupassant*

"Bill Ballance certainly writes with a Facile Pen."—*Frederick Facile*

"A diabolic masterpiece—this bloody book is harder to put down than a tray in a busy cafeteria."—*Mary Wollstonecraft*

"Ballance's astringent satire pokes holes in stuffed shirts, through which the sawdust slowly trickles."—*Anthony Trollope*

"Ballance is no longer a disk jockey, now he is a radio host, and the host is to the DJ what the lapidary is to the bricklayer. To have him on the air five hours a day is Paradise Regained." —*John Milton*

"Nasty criticism of Ballance? Blast it, we should all forget niggling critics . . . to go through life living off other people's works must have an incredibly degrading effect on them and let us hope that it's not the amorphous shape of things to come."—*H. G. Wells*

"Life is good literature escaping; good literature is life held fast. And when I'm fasting, I prefer the nutritious works of Bill Ballance."—*Mahatma Gandhi*

"Whew, Ballance has committed a book written in a light vein that somehow becomes vericose. Of course don't take me too seriously because my mission in life is to pour high-test vinegar on troubled authors."—*Santayana*

"Ballance should never worry about being put down by critics. Literary criticism has no serious value except perhaps as an expression of the critic's inane philosophy."—*William Dean Howells*

"This is a book for people with a desire to know, for those who are seeking the reason why, for those with a zest to know the truth."—*Dean Jonathan Swift*

"Ballance writes with luminous directness; the clarity and precision of his word choice, full of subtle turns, makes him intensely readable."—*Steve and Butterfly McQueen* as observed to *Patti* and *Satchel Paige*

"Why do I prefer Ballance's books to television? Because they're not always interrupting themselves to tell me to go out and buy something."—*Guglielmo Marconi*

"I suspect that Ballance thinks bubblegum cards are part of my Great Books series."—*Mortimer Adler*

"Ballance's wit rises fresh between semi-colons; his paradoxes are used like shortcut definitions to elaborate truths. His English is unsurpassed for mastery of style, vocabulary, and innovation; his prose is bright, concise, and in the vernacular. I don't know how the hell he does it."—*John P. Marquand*

"After reading Ballance, all I can say is La Rochefoucauld had better look to his Maximal laurels."—*B. Traven*

"Ballance writes about contemporary life felicitously, in lucid and persuasive expository prose; there's a live nervous system pulsing in every sentence, for he is relentlessly amusing, he never lets up. He is able to cement abstract words together with a thick mortar of dependent and parenthetical clauses, producing a bulwark of impenetrable prose."—*James Russell Lowell* in collaboration with *Michel Eyquem, Seigneur de Montaigne*

"A book is like a woman. If the outside is deftly decorative without too much show of intellectual depth, it sells. So how can Ballance miss?"—*William Faulkner*

"No matter how busy you may think you are, you must find time for reading, or surrender yourself to self-chosen ignorance. You can accomplish both by reading Ballance."—*Oliver Wendell Holmes*

"Occasionally there emerges a book which is a lighthouse erected in the great sea of time, so it is now essential to point out that Ballance is no beacon."—*Joseph Conrad*

"I prefer books over television. Books are calm; they never dissolve into wavy lines or flopovers. Books never pause to deliver a message from their sponsor. Books are three dimensional, possessing length, breadth, and depth, and they are completely portable. So I think it's likely that Ballance will soon be on television."—*Lady Nancy Astor*

"Ballance's work is like a patient on the operating table who has gallstones, liver problems, various tumors and digestive disorders. It's interesting no matter where you open it up."—*Edgar Allen Poe*

"Wonder is the beginning of wisdom, in learning from books as well as from Nature. If you never ask yourself any questions about the meaning of a paragraph, you cannot expect the book to give you any insight that you do not already possess, so all I can say to you is—if you fail to read Ballance—*tough taco.*" *—Emiliano Zapata*

"Each book that you read plays its part in carving your character. You can live in the company of the great and share their thoughts, so I think it's a shame about certain presumptuous broadcasters."*—Herman Melville*

"What we don't dare print is precisely what people want to read; hence you have my secret and confidential imprimatur to absorb the Best of Ballance."*—Noah Webster*

"Ballance's writing is blessed with absolute pitch. He uses words as a lens to give life and depth to the characters and landscape of a distant and now abstruse period of history. It is no surprise that this superb piece of historical portraiture has lasted to this year, 2315."*—Garson Kanin XII,* Founder of Lackluster Library Touch 'N' Tell Instant Absorption Books

"Ballance is fascinated by the proper rhythm and order of words and he seizes all opportunities for their contemplation. He then displays considerable rhetorical flourish on his low road to wordly wisdom, for, indeed, a poor appetite for books eventually leads to intellectual malnutrition. If this is true, he's now in training for a famine. But it all adds up to splendid fun during the lonesome watches of your sleepless nights. . . . If to write is a desire for redemption, Ballance's Day has just arrived."*—Anton Chekhov*

"During his hyper-active life, Ballance-Hotep accumulated several pyramids of notes, papery paraphernalia of scholarship; his illuminated scrolls now decorate the tombs of my ancestors (you'll recall his classic: *How Egyptian Mummifiers Mastered the Art of Making a Woman Dry Up and Stay that Way*), and my advisors are now negotiating with his descendants for a little something for me to take along into Eternity, for I don't intend to be alone out there without his Jocular Jottings."*—Rameses II*

"Ballance has condensed a lifetime's reading and thought into a brilliant, concise, and remarkable clear-headed appraisal of these chaotic days, revealing that same organized wit and insight that make his daily shows the most listenable of our time. He's a real kick in the gonads."—*Arthur Conan Doyle* as told to *Norman Mailer* through a Spirit Medium

"A book is a success when people who haven't read it pretend they have. That's why Ballance has me pretending as I never have before."—*Epictetus* during sly exchange with Aeschylus

"I can imagine BB struggling inkily with this, his first book, a valiant word-splurge. He's no Hemingway, but he is Ernest." —*H. L. Mencken*

"The writings of the Wise are the only riches our Posterity cannot squander—so I must emphasize that BB is a writer well worth watching. Not reading, just watching."—*William Lyon Phelps*

"To praise someone whose rivalry you do not dread is a splendid way of putting a spoke in the wheel of someone whose rivalry you do; hence, I regard Ballance's balderdash as the Wave of the Future."—*The Duke of Wellington* as remarked to Fred Talleyrand.

"BB is an athlete of images; he performs alchemy with words on his radio programs that brings out their overtones, their most utter value for evocation of persuasive charm, displaying considerable verbal acuity. This is why I submit that he is destined to become the world's most widely unknown successful author. While monitoring his top-rated broadcasts, I have analyzed his inflections with elocutionary zeal and found him wanton."—*Leo Tolstoy*

"The dynamic movement of human beings through Time, Space, and Circumstance is fluently described by Ballance, but what pleases me most is that in his entire book there's not a single exclamation point. There are a few *chilly italics*, but I've always felt that an exclamation point is like laughing at your own joke."—*Elbert Hubbard*

"The critics will crucify BB. He should ignore them; no one should fear criticism. Anyone who can fill out a laundry slip thinks of himself as a writer. Those who can't fill out a laundry slip think of themselves as critics."—*Samuel Langhorn Clemens*

"Ballance is a man of prodigious creative powers and supple mind; his writing has clarity, brevity, lucidity. Just one thing—it doesn't make sense."—*Geoffrey Chaucer*

"The secret of writing is to learn big words and then learn *not* to use them. Writing is simply the writer and the reader on opposite ends of a pencil. They should be as close together as that; so let me say that it is obvious that Ballance is pitching overhand at his Underwood."—*Dizzy Dean*

"Ballance wrote this book under an assumed name. He's calling himself an author."—*Sir Francis Bacon*

"I guess Ballance is OK, but his book isn't exactly a fortress of grammatical exactitude. If Bill Buckley hadn't copyrighted the term, I'd say it's a lot of crap."—*Gertrude Stein*

"Autobiographies are meaningless because no man dares put into writing the most significant facts of his life. Writers of autobiographies leave out the details you would most like to know about. All they give you is a few gamy epithets and slanted 'facts' on how they want you to think they lived. I anticipate Ballance's mendacious memoirs more than somewhat; there will be no doctrinal dilution. He might even win the Nobel Prize for Penmanship."—*Ernest Thompson Seton* as told to Albert Payson Terhune while basting Bambi at a Sequoia cookout

"Ballance is bound to attract a cult with worldwide ramifications, and anyone who disagrees with his precepts must be motived by villainy alone. Of this I am certain. But I am not quite sure what he is saying in his colorful way; I reread his comments and each time come up with different meanings. Let me put it this way—from the dew of those flakes that melted on my face, I cannot reconstruct the snowstorm."—*Walt Whitman*

"To write a book takes stamina, resolution, and discipline; Ballance writes like O'Hara, and I'll bet you didn't know Maureen could write."—*John Wayne*

"In this book, Ballance is lusting after the polished phrase; his prose is bright, concise and in the vernacular. He reminds me of Alexander King, the junkie Mark Twain. In real life, he must be as lecherous as a monkey. And where does he get off, issuing all those Laws?"—*Hammurabi*

"Ballance is professionally ambidextrous; a natural performer, an excellent writer—gifts rarely combined in one person. My envy of him makes my eye turn outward."—*Aldous Huxley*

"Listen, I love Ballance's work so much that if I don't get a personally inscribed first edition of his superb book, I will fling myself into the river."—*Virginia Woolf*

"This is not a book to be tossed lightly aside. It should be thrown with great force."—*Dashiell Hammett*

"Bill Ballance has condensed a lifetime's reading and thought into a remarkably clear-headed appraisal of our times; his work is rich in illuminating insights and genial wisdom. If he were an animal, I'd have him immortalized on film."—*Walt Disney* on the back of a David O. Selznick memo

"Ballance's first book is slapdash, slipshod, murky in logic, sloppily annotated, useless for reference, and fun to read."—*J. R. R. Tolkien*

"With sardonic eye and urbane pen, Ballance produces readable, mosaic prose; hardly anyone knows that this captivating codger writes with a 200-year-old quill and shakes grains of sand onto the parchment to dry his homemade ink. But somehow, in a shifting foreground of misplaced time and mistimed space, he tells it all in this perky work."—*Franz Kafka*

"Ballance is an author of power and glittering malice, blatantly aphrodisiacal in intent, profoundly humorous in content. He writes with a forceful combination of personal journalism and disciplined documentation. This is his finest work since 'The Greening of an Olive.' "—*Havelock Ellis*

"The only thing worse than a man with one book is a man with one book he hasn't read. Well, I have Ballance's first effort here and I'll get to it as soon as I finish this tunnel."—*The Count of Monte Cristo*

"Ballance is caught up by the cataract of history, true, but he is only a snipe pretending to be an eagle. I suspect he's a closet elitist."—*Edmund Wilson*

"This First Folio of Ballance doth intrigue mightily the likes of me."—*John Donne*

"Ballance writes books with imagination—he imagines people read them. The nicest, most kindly thing I can say about him is that his work is a tasteless clot of campy tampering."—*Hermann Hesse*

"Outside a dog, a man's best friend is a book; inside a dog, you can't read a book anyway. But if you could, I would recommend Ballance. In every work of genius, we recognize our own rejected thoughts; they come back to us with a certain alienated majesty, and that's swell."—*Kahlil Gibran*

"The covers of Ballance's book are too far apart."—*Johann Gutenberg*

Concluding Remarks by the Beloved Author and a Little Shameless Promotion for His Next Project

Here I am, dug into the middle of all my books and papers, snug as a silverfish, crooning to myself like a bilious pigeon, piecing together my autobiography. I'm not doing it voluntarily, I'm doing it at the behest of my eager publisher, Nash—The Literary Titans. These memoirs, which I intend to publish posthumously—if I should live that long—will be called *Events Leading Up to My Death in the Year 2025.* Like late election returns, posthumous books rarely turn the tide of opinion for or against a man. Because my life is one long reflex improvisation, I'm tempted to call it *Total Recoil,* for I am writing it with the passionate intensity of a man plucking shell fragments out of his memory. Most autobiographies are long-winded, self-caressing ruminations full of bloated rhetoric and mundane memorabilia. They read like a brief for canonization; they're a verbal orgy of nostalgic egomania. The author is trying to explore his own existence, to relate himself to what has happened to him and how he's reacted. He is, by writing his autobiography, setting his life in order, probably for the first time; hence the unique function of autobiography is to flaunt *form* as it's being constructed from *chaos.*

So as I bash out my memoirs on this rickety Selectric, I hereby promise not to bore the living kapok out of you with golden reminiscences of my dear, dead childhood. An honest, straight-on autobiography is a personal, lopsided, idiosyncratic kind of manual which tells far more about a man than any conventional alibiography or apologia; and it's far better than a diary, which is nothing more than the slightly organized debris of a man's life. Most autobiographies should be titled *The Manly Art of Self-Deception,* because they are masterpieces of self-concealment. They are, however, unrivaled vehicles for telling the truth about *other* people. I want the world to accept my autobiog as confidential truth; so watch for my meticulous, rueful reflections and remember Ballance's Law of Absorption: The well-read person is called cultured, not because he possesses a fund of charming but useless expressions, but rather because he has acquired a lifetime tenancy in a constantly growing share of the accumulated experience of the race.

That's It.

About the Author

Bill Ballance's mental agility has been honed to a high gloss by a lifetime of professional preparation for his daily five-hour broadcasts—now performed before a live audience in the KGBS-Storer Radio Star Theater at Universal Studios, Hollywood. A broadcaster since he was seventeen, he is currently in his fifth year at KGBS, Los Angeles. This was preceded by a stint at KNBR, San Francisco; a decade at KFWB, Hollywood; three years at KNX, Hollywood; KGIL, San Fernando; KHVH, Honolulu, Hawaii; WBKB-TV, Chicago; six years at KOA, Denver. He is a graduate of the University of Illinois in journalism and was a combat officer in the Marine Corps, ending his service as a captain. Ballance's captivating daily show is not only syndicated internationally, but will be going before the TV cameras (titled "Off-Ballance") as this book goes to press. Bill has been divorced twice and is the father of two grown sons, Jim and Kurt. He revels in his life as a roving Hollywood bachelor and in owning and operating a free-lance heart, the cockles of which he warms regularly to avoid being cold cockled.